The Whole
Enchilada

OTHER MARKETING BOOKS FROM PMP

The Whole Enchilada

Hispanic Marketing 101

Juan Faura

PMP

PARAMOUNT MARKET PUBLISHING, INC.

Paramount Market Publishing, Inc.
301 S. Geneva Street, Suite 109
Ithaca, NY 14850
www.paramountbooks.com
Telephone: 607-275-8100; 888-787-8100   Facsimile: 607-275-8101

Publisher: James Madden
Editorial Director: Doris Walsh

Cataloging in Publication Data available
ISBN 0-9725290-5-5

Book design and composition: Paperwork

Contents

For Sara, Juan, Amanda and Sebastian.
You are my life.

Foreword

I t was August 2002 and I had just returned from a five-week sabbatical, much needed after 11 years of service with one of the leading brands in the world. Just eighteen months earlier I had accepted a new role within the company that had quickly evolved into two distinct jobs, which was nothing new in this company and my career.

The first job was responsible for managing a significant part of our footwear sales business and the other focused on understanding sport and today's multicultural youth. My mind was feeling clear and fresh from the break, at least for a while, which was essential because I was hoping to bring some clarity to this thing called the Hispanic market, the pinnacle of today's multicultural youth.

I had attended conferences, talked to various agencies and experts in the marketplace. I had been provided enough stats, charts, demographics, and power point presentations to sink a small boat. Even with all that data at my fingertips there still was something not right, at least to me. I kept telling myself the Hispanic market can't be this boring, this limited, or this "cheesy."

I was heading to a Hispanic youth conference being held in San Diego. Although I was tired of the conference scene, this conference promised it would be a small gathering of experts in the industry with specific focus on Hispanic youth. One of the frustrations with the Hispanic industry is that it had not yet distinguished the difference between the Hispanic youth market and the entire marketplace. All the discussions were just around the entire market and how it needed to be addressed. Because of this, most industry professionals and experts would get stuck reveling in three topics: the Census data, generalizations about the market, and the infamous "language" debate.

Fortunately for me, this conference would live up to its promise. It was at the conference in San Diego where Juan Faura and I met for the first time and where I would finally see him present. Later that same day I described him face to face as "The Serpico of the Hispanic Market." I just kept thinking of Al Pacino in his different outfits trying to tell anyone who would listen how things really were.

Juan was one of a small handful of people in the industry that talked from a consumer's point of view and not the Hispanic marketing and media industries' point of view. He screamed consumer and provided a sense of street credibility. His insights were pure and interactive. It was less about the fancy graphic and more about the stories behind the data the created the fancy graphic. He told you what he heard and what he saw without putting a self-serving editorial spin to it. His physical appearance also provided a sense of assurance, as he would look as comfortable leaning against a wall in East LA as he would against a wall in a corporate boardroom. He was a reflection of the consumer in the marketplace.

As I listened to Juan's presentation, I reflected on one of the highlights of my sabbatical—the eleven days I visited El Salvador to see family and spent time with many cousins. They were cousins whose ages ranged from 14 to 30 years old. I hadn't seen most of them for years, but it took only 10 minutes to be "familia" once again. But what was significant about the experience was no matter how much my cousins and I had in common they looked at the world through a different lens than I did.

They were raised in El Salvador and I was raised in the United States, a simple fact that despite all our shared blood, culture, and grandparents still distinguished us. This obvious difference had become the clarity I was seeking.

Most companies come to two conclusions when looking at the Hispanic market. Either they do nothing because they conclude most Latinos eventually want to be American and "buy American" and over time they will come to their brand. Or they approach the market in a traditional way and do everything in Spanish because most Latinos want what they had back in their country of origin.

As you will find out from Juan and others like him neither is true. Hispanic/Latinos have much more to offer and the industry is selling their marketplace and themselves short. However for the Hispanic industry, this approach made complete sense in the past. As a Hispanic marketing, advertising or media agency you needed to distinguish yourself from the general market and hustle to obtain those hard to come by advertising dollars. But for the consumer and the marketplace this was a very short sighted and narrow view. The marketplace has changed and the consumer has changed. The general market no longer exists and multiculturalism has become a reality and the Hispanic consumer its first pure example.

Hispanic consumers are now living in the two worlds that make up their culture, American and Latino, and do not have to give up either one, or define which one is more important. Companies, directors, and some researchers want them to make this choice because it would make our lives easier. Today's multicultural consumer doesn't have to choose. Yet the industry continues to try to oversimplify a marketplace that is dynamic, accessible, and user friendly.

As you read Juan's book and he walks you through some of the practical elements you will need to address the market, I hope you are able to enter with a clear and open mind. If there is one thing the book makes clear, it is that this is not rocket science and you do not have to have an MBA to be successful selling to them.

I also hope you will get the essence of what the book is about.

Hispanics come in all flavors and colors and if you are going to be successful selling to them you need to understand that. I don't think you have to go on a sabbatical to achieve this, but if you need an excuse to take a few days off you have one now. There is a group of us in the industry that believes the Hispanic consumer that you are about to learn about brings so much more to the table, even beyond the buying dollars you have heard so much about. That is why you bought the book, isn't it? Their appeal to companies in the U.S. has gone beyond a Spanish version of other youth, or naive immigrants with limited dollars and the desire for anything you can give away as a sample. (Gratis! Gratis! Gratis!)

Instead we think it's about the balance of respecting tradition and culture, but not letting tradition restrain you and the future. We also think it is about having more not fewer people consider this market an opportunity to grow and sustain their business.

ED ARCE
Director of Multicultural Business
Nike, Inc.

Preface

I actually wrote three versions of the preface to this book. Every time I wrote one, I thought I had nailed it. And then I read it and was totally disappointed. The very reason for writing this book was to demystify marketing to U.S. Hispanic consumers for the everyday businessperson, and I felt none of the prefaces I had written really "nut-shelled" the idea. There are so many books and articles and essays and briefs on the subject that approach it in a very complete, but very dry and complicated, way that I believe many people are turned off to the opportunity. So I set out to write something for the small businessperson who has no experience or background marketing to Hispanics.

Throughout the book, I try to maintain this conversational and, I hope, easy-to-read tone. I do, however, have to apologize for those instances (and there are probably several) in which I revert to the ethnotechnical jargon so beloved by those of us who make our living in this field. I also have to apologize to those who make a living by convincing their clients that they could not possibly understand this market because they themselves are not Hispanic. I feel like I am pulling back the curtain on the Wizard of Oz. And in no way do I exempt myself from this group, either. I too, in an earlier and less enlightened life, spoke from behind the curtain and told all who were interested, "I know it because they are my people, and you don't because they are not your people." So all cultural shamans should feel free to write their own books.

Obviously, I'm being sarcastic, but the fact of the matter is that the time has come for the formula to be revealed. What you will read in this book is the nuts and bolts of marketing to Hispanic consumers—nothing more, nothing less. I am not providing social commentary or a point of view on what the value of the Hispanic consumer is for your business. I am merely trying to help you get more out of your business by better understanding your Hispanic customers and potential customers.

Don't get me wrong; there is a very spiritual and esoteric aspect to the Hispanic culture, one that cannot be quantified or defined. There is a richness and flavor to the culture, just as there is in every other culture. The point, though, is that you don't necessarily have to understand all of this to be successful selling to Hispanic consumers. You need to understand certain practical aspects that this book is meant to address.

JUAN FAURA
Dallas, Texas

Acknowledgments

I always wondered whether the authors of the books I read really needed everybody in the acknowledgments or whether they were just covering their butts and mentioning everyone they knew. Now I know you really do need all those people. If you are Hispanic you will completely understand the order the first three are in!

My mother, Elvia, *gracias por darme vida*. My wife, Sara, thanks for putting up with me. My brother, Roque, for the late-night tacos. Mary Hardesty, thank you for your friendship, sage advice, and guidance. Alex Campo, your art direction made the original the book as friendly as I intended it to be. Halim "Media Master" Trujillo, thank you for all the numbers and no I am not mad at you. Gabriel and David Garcia, thanks for keeping me honest. Greg Knipp, thanks for sharing your perspective and insight into the Hispanic opportunity. Ed Arce, for being a kindred spirit. My Cultura family, you guys are an inspiration every day. Arturo Del Villar, thank you for the research piece. Tony Dieste and Warren Harmel for raising the bar. And to all my *paisanos* that have gotten here on a wing and a prayer and are making it happen every day, you make me proud to be Mexican.

The Eight Laws of the Hispanic Universe

1 Culture is about more than language. Talk to us in our culture, and the language thing will come.

2 Assume we will be emotional and dramatic; it makes things like relationships easier, and brings flavor to life.

3 When you are at a Hispanic friend's house—and it doesn't matter how old you are by the way—and their mom offers you food, do not refuse a plate (not that you will be able to anyway).

4 Sound remains in the brain longer. For us, that sound needs to be music.

5 Intellect and Emotion are partners who do not speak the same language. Emotion is the key to our hearts.

6 Family is always first. Family means your mom and dad and brothers and sisters and cousins and second cousins and cousins of your aunt's husband's sister and aunts of your mom's second cousin Dionisia from Veracruz.

7 Disposition will always outweigh ability. If we want something enough, we will figure out a way to buy it. We do not limit our dreams; why should you?

8 We are dramatic and loud and exaggerated. It is part of what brings flavor to our culture, and we love it.

How the Hispanic Market Is Changing

As anyone who came from Mexico prior to 1990 can tell you, the number of "American" brands and products available in Mexico was once a tiny fraction of what it is today. Immigrants coming into the U.S. marketplace were presented with new brands and products across all categories. For most Hispanics coming from Mexico, almost every single category, from packaged goods to automotive, was underdeveloped. Companies needed to first inform and educate the consumer about their product or brand, since there was no equity in either for these consumers. Anyone who has been to Mexico in the past year can tell you that the shopping scene has changed dramatically.

From packaged goods to fast food to automotive, the Mexican marketplace is now a virtual mirror to what we experience here in the U.S. Wal-Mart, Costco, and Target dot the Mexican retail landscape. McDonald's, Pizza Hut, Domino's, and Taco Bell are but a few of the fast-food companies now operating in Mexico.

This change has affected how the U.S. Hispanic marketplace has evolved. Countless conversations with research professionals who make their living by recruiting Hispanics for marketing studies have only confirmed what should, by now, have been obvious. Today's Hispanic consumers are vastly different from Hispanic consumers of five years ago. They are more sophisticated from a category standpoint. They have been exposed to cutting-edge, in-language-marketing communications, and they have begun to demand more from those companies that want to communicate with them.

The notion that U.S. Hispanic consumers are what general market consumers were in the 1950s is a comfortable oversimplification that grossly misses the more significant opportunity. This opportunity is there not only for big corporations, but also for small businesses all across the United States. Although the complexity of the effort will be dramatically different, small businesses have taken and continue to take advantage of the growth in the U.S. Hispanic population.

The bottom line is that whether a company has marketed to the Hispanic market over the years or is only now turning its attention to this market, it will find the Hispanic market is a recognized area for incremental sales, volume growth, and market-share acquisition. In the next chapters, I hope you will find that valuable nugget of inspiration that will lead you to embark on a treacherous but wonderful journey into a culture that has long been a part of the fabric of Americana but is only now beginning to get the recognition it deserves.

Some Key Numbers

Before we go further, let's take a quick look at some key numbers. As of June 2003 the U.S. Hispanic population was 38.8 million, including Puerto Rico. Mexicans make up about 67 percent of the U.S. Hispanic population, Central and South Americans 13 percent, Puerto Ricans 10 percent, Cubans 4 percent, and other Hispanic 6 percent. I say "about" because the figures vary depending on the source. Suffice it to say that for our purposes these numbers give you the makeup of the population. One interesting tidbit that I think is worth mentioning is that the Hispanic population in Chicago reflects the mixture of the country. That is to say, the Hispanic population of Chicago is roughly 65 percent Mexican, 20 percent Puerto Rican, and 15 percent South and Central American.

Age

The U.S. Hispanic population is younger than the at-large population. The average age of the Hispanic population is 28, compared with 34 for the population at large. What this means from a communication standpoint is that you need to consider a younger audience when you think about what you are going to say. That may mean that you should be more contemporary or modern with what you say, or it may also mean that you will find a more receptive market for products or services aimed at a population that is coming of age, rather than aging. Of course all of this will need to be balanced with cultural norms that are a part of the Hispanic culture. Generally speaking, Hispanics tend to be a bit more conservative in values and customs, which means that although they are a younger market, they can also be more conservative than other comparably aged markets.

Population Growth

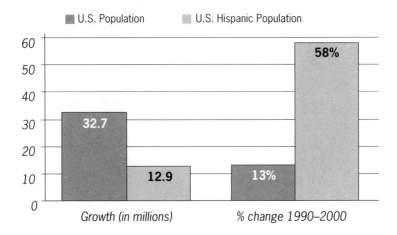

The following charts will provide you with basic demographic data. They are based on 2000 census figures. You are probably saying to yourself, "2000. Aren't those figures outdated?" The answer is yes, but for our purposes they are as accurate as they need to be. For more up-to-date numbers you can access the U.S. Census website (www.census.gov). It is a complete and reliable source of information. Truth be told, for those of you who are small-business owners or managers, these figures will not play a practical role in your efforts, but they will help you keep the larger picture in mind

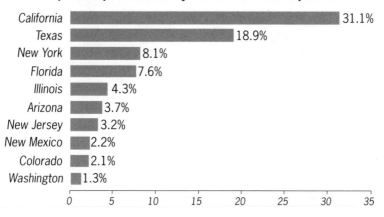

Top 10 States by Hispanic Population

in millions

California	11.0
Texas	6.7
New York	2.9
Florida	2.7
Illinois	1.6
Arizona	1.3
New Jersey	1.1
New Mexico	0.8
Colorado	0.7
Washington	0.4

Top 10 Hispanic States by Percent of Total Hispanics

California	31.1%
Texas	18.9%
New York	8.1%
Florida	7.6%
Illinois	4.3%
Arizona	3.7%
New Jersey	3.2%
New Mexico	2.2%
Colorado	2.1%
Washington	1.3%

2

Why the Hispanic Market?

Unless you have been living under a rock for the past couple of years, you have heard about the incredible growth in the U.S. Hispanic population. For those of you who have in fact lived under a rock, try these numbers on for size: The Hispanic population in the U.S .is the second-largest population behind the white, non-Hispanic population. It makes up almost 14 percent of the overall population of the United States. Hispanics are now the largest population group in Los Angeles. In Miami, Hispanic median household income is higher than that of the general market.

Still not impressed? Hispanics are younger overall, with a median age of 28 compared with a median age for the rest of the population of 34. This market segment is growing at six times the rate of all other populations combined. The growth is due to immigration and a higher birth rate. Hispanic households are inherently larger than those in the overall population.

For these and other reasons I will outline, the U.S. Hispanic market represents the future of many companies in the United States. Aside from its sheer size, the Hispanic market is an extremely attractive business proposition because Hispanics are clustered in a definable number of markets. As you will see, if you were to market to Hispanics in the Top 10 Hispanic markets outlined in Chapter 1 you would be marketing to over 50 percent of the Hispanic population!

If you are a company that operates on a national level you can, in fact, target half of the U.S. Hispanic population if you include just Texas and California in your marketing plan. As a group U.S. Hispanics wield more than $600 billion in buying power. Projections by The Selig Center at the University of Georgia are that Hispanic buying power will reach more than $1 trillion by 2008.

The growth of the Hispanic population and its economic strength has not gone unnoticed. Many major companies in the U.S., including Fortune 100 companies, are hard at work trying to tap into this lucrative market. Unfortunately, many of them are wasting a lot of money because they do not know the basic approach to targeting these consumers. As I mentioned before, the idea behind this book is to teach you how to target this lucrative market in very practical and workable terms. Whether you are a billion-dollar multinational corporation or a small neighborhood business, you will be able to target the market more effectively. Since many of the techniques and much of the information in this book have to do with "on the ground" tactical elements, I would argue that the book will prove to be more fruitful to the smaller-business owner.

If you are a company that operates on a national level you can target half of the U.S. Hispanic population if you include just Texas and California in your marketing plan.

Ultimately I wanted to write something easy to read and easy to understand for someone with absolutely no experience in marketing to U.S. Hispanics. I think that what follows has achieved this goal. I also think that even for those of you with significant experience marketing to U.S. Hispanics, the information in this book, which is most likely familiar to you, will be presented in a new and fresh way. I hope it inspires you either way.

The book is designed in a modular format. This means that you can use any of the modules independent of the others as needed. This was done for two reasons: First, without knowing your specific business scenario, I cannot come up with a specific solution for targeting the Hispanic market, but I can provide you with a "tool box" that you can use as you need. Second, since the book is meant to address the Hispanic market regardless of the type of business you are running, some of its components will not be relevant to small-business owners and some will not be relevant to large multinationals. Regardless of the type of company you operate, the information contained is meant to make you more savvy about marketing to U.S. Hispanic consumers.

What This Book Is and Is Not

In all fairness, I think before we get too far I should let you know what this book is not. It is not a deep analysis of the U.S. Hispanic market. You will not find an in-depth overview of the Hispanic culture either. What this book is meant to be is a no-nonsense guide from A to Z for marketing to the U.S. Hispanic market. There are plenty of conferences, books and companies looking to provide anyone willing to listen with insights on the Hispanic mindset, culture, and demographics.

While this book will include some demographic data, it is not based on it. Every component of this book is meant to provide the reader with a very tactical "how to" for every aspect of marketing to the Hispanic market. Although this book can easily serve as a roadmap to Hispanic marketing for small- to medium-size companies, large-scale initiatives will require that you partner with people who dedicate themselves to communicating with this market. If you work for a large or multinational company you most likely know that already. If you will need to partner with a specialized company I hope this book will serve as a guide to making an intelligent and informed decision.

3

Getting Started

O ne of the first things you will need to do, regardless of the size and scope of your company, is decide that you are going to make a concerted effort to tap into the Hispanic market. That may seem obvious to you, but believe me, if you do not make the conscious decision and commitment to do it, your efforts will end up being just another attempt at getting more customers through your doors, right along with the weekly flyer on the windshield or coupon on the door hanger.

This needs to be a conscious decision, because if you are going to be truly successful, you have to approach the market with a long-term commitment. Now, that does not mean that you may not begin to reap the rewards right away, but you need to be ready for an ongoing effort. Believe me, it will be worth it. For a small business this should actually be relatively simple. With fewer employees, you should be able to instill in all of them the idea that they will benefit by increased sales and the long-term success of the business. In a small-business environment it will be precisely those employees, the people behind the counter, who make your Hispanic initiative successful.

About Hispanics

Most ad agencies, research companies, marketing companies and promotions companies look to gain clients for Hispanic-market campaigns by demonstrating how well they know the Hispanic culture. At every single conference I have ever attended, either as a delegate or a speaker, each presentation attempts to give the audience a unique perspective or insight on the market. Like any other population on the planet, Hispanics in the U.S. have certain characteristics that are particular to their culture. As I said earlier, this is true of every culture, not only the Hispanic culture. That includes people over age 50, teenagers, Harley-Davidson riders, etc. Each of these groups is a defined culture with traits particular to it. Obviously, some are more unique than others. When it comes to the Hispanic culture, there are as many hues as there are in the at-large population. For some reason, however, marketers think that in order to market to the Hispanic population you have to fully understand all of its nuances. That couldn't be further from the truth.

> *When it comes to the Hispanic culture, there are as many hues as there are in the at-large population.*

Although the success of marketing to any group of people will correlate to our understanding of that group, it is not absolutely necessary that we understand everything about that group in order to market to it, particularly when we are talking about marketing on a smaller scale. Nevertheless, I will look to provide you with the insights about the culture that you will need to market to them successfully.

One of the questions I get most often is whether people like to be referred to as Hispanic or as Latino. The answer to that is that you can go either way without offending anyone. Most of the studies and surveys I have seen or heard about indicate that the population prefers Hispanic, but as I said, you will not offend anyone if you use Latino.

And since we are on the subject, what defines someone as a Hispanic or Latino? The census has specific criteria that must be met. (For simplicity's sake, since it was the census that first began using Hispanic to describe the population, we will stick with Hispanic.) One of the most important criteria is self-identification: How do people define themselves? That is the criteria most often used for research, and it is the criteria we will use. The way I see it, if someone believes he or she is Hispanic, then for our purposes, he or she is Hispanic.

Stereotypes

As we all know, stereotypes are usually based on true aspects of a culture, a belief, or ethnic values. They are exaggerations and generalizations of those truths. This is also true of the U.S. Hispanic culture. Many U.S. multinational corporations, small businesses, and single operators alike make business determinations based on erroneous stereotypes and perceptions, often generated by completely outdated cultural models and perpetuated by Hollywood.

Certain Hispanic ad and marketing agencies and research companies also perpetuate stereotypes, but they do it out of a sense of self-preservation. By maintaining a static cultural model, these agencies seek to ensure their place as the experts. The perception is that if the U.S. Hispanic consumer is seen as being as evolved as the U.S. general market consumer, it would mean a significant erosion of the value that multicultural agencies bring to the party.

The reality is that an evolved consumer will require, more than ever, a culturally savvy partner willing to move to the leading edge of cultural evolution. This, in my opinion, means a significant opportunity for Hispanic marketing thought leaders and the demise of those who rely on cultural shamanism. First, let's go over some of what you will most likely hear time and again about Hispanics from ad agencies, and marketing or research companies:

- **Hispanics are driven by their families. Their whole world revolves around family.**

- Hispanics are very literal. They will take everything you say at face value.

- Hispanics are brand-loyal. Once they use a brand they stick with it.

- Hispanics are warm people. They prefer a hug to a hand-shake.

- Hispanics have very defined gender roles within the household.

- Hispanic moms don't like to use ready-made or instant products. They like to make everything from scratch.

- Hispanic parents do not like to see their children dirty or unkempt. You can't show kids getting dirty with their moms watching, even if the kids are having fun.

- You shouldn't portray single-parent families when communicating with Hispanic consumers.

- Hispanics love salsa music. Hispanics love their cars.

- Hispanics love bright colors.

While some of these assumptions might be true, a number of them are outdated, while still others are flat-out wrong. The connection between these cultural nuggets and actual purchase behavior or how to affect that behavior is tenuous at best.

Let's consider the following example: Hispanic moms, generally speaking, like to take care of their family first. They therefore prefer to cook from scratch and not use instant or fast food. This information would lead us to believe that a company, like Kraft Foods with its Macaroni & Cheese, Kool-Aid, and Tang, would consider Hispanics a difficult market to crack. This couldn't be further from the truth. In fact, Kraft Foods is one of the top multinational companies marketing precisely those products to those moms.

So what gives? Culturally Hispanics are not predisposed to use the products, yet the manufacturers of the products are investing money to win their loyalty. What is happening is that what people are told about U.S. Hispanic moms is only half right.

Those cultural insights are true, but no consumer operates in a vacuum; there is a context to the culture—a practical, functional context. U.S. Hispanic moms are entering the workforce in record numbers. They are starting their own businesses in order to help provide for the household. They are doing this and still trying to take care of their families.

Since they do not live in an alternate universe where time stretches, today's Hispanic moms know that concessions have to be made. Convenience is the most obvious, and one that they can actually do something to feel better about. Mom will cook the Kraft Macaroni & Cheese, but may add her own recipe for *picadillo* (a spicy dish made with ground beef). By doing that, she has made it her own meal. She feels good because she prepared it and incorporated her own touch.

In the next few chapters we will discuss who U.S. Hispanic customers or clients really are. By this, I mean who they really are as people, as parents, as sons and daughters—where they come from, and what their lives are all about.

I figured the best way to do that would be to introduce you to a few of the people who will be working for you or hiring you, buying your products, or walking into your store. You will meet a selected group of people, males and females of all ages, educational levels and stages of acculturation. Each of these people, made from a composite of actual people, represents the varied and rich hues that make up the tapestry of the U.S. Hispanic culture. So without further ado, let me introduce you to some of my friends and your future customers.

4

Mucho Gusto*
(It's a pleasure to meet you)

Ana María Gonzalez, Age 22, Los Angeles CA

Hello, my name is Ana María Gonzalez, and I live in Los Angeles. I was actually born in Sacramento, but I moved down here with parents and my brothers when I was three. My dad is originally from Puebla, Mexico, and he has been here 23 years. He speaks enough English to get by, but at home he speaks only Spanish. My mom is from Guatemala. She speaks even less English than my father, even though she has been taking English classes at the night school for more than 15 years. Now that I think about it all of the women that take the classes with her have been doing it for that long, and none of them speaks English.

I can speak Spanish fluently, although I know it isn't perfect. I know that sometimes I have to use "pochismos," which is when I can't think of the right word in Spanish, so I make it up using the word in English. Like the other day I was trying to remember how to say "parking" in Spanish because I was trying to tell Lorena's mom that's where I was going. I couldn't remember it is *estacionar* in Spanish, so I just said *parkear*. I also use "Spanglish" when I talk to my friends. Spanglish is when I start a sentence in English and then also use Spanish words in the same sentence. It isn't something we plan or think about, you know, it is just how

---

* Portraits presented here are composites of people I know. None is intended to represent a particular person.

we talk, how it flows. I am finishing my second year in junior college and I am hoping to transfer to San Luis Obispo next fall.

We live by Echo Park, which is a not-so-nice area of Los Angeles. There are drugs and gangs and other things that I imagine are a part of any big city. Right now I am working part time at a small handbag factory here in town, but I hope to eventually get my teaching credential and teach high school. In my spare time, which isn't a lot, I help my mom with the house and with my youngest brother. I also like hanging out with my friends from the neighborhood and going to parties, although now I have to be more careful about the parties I go to. Marissa, this friend of mine, was actually caught in a drive-by shooting the other day. Nothing happened to her, but she was scared to death.

I like—no, I love—to listen to the radio. I listen to it on the bus, in my room, in the car, everywhere. What do I like to listen to? The question is *what don't I like* to listen to? I like R&B and hip-hop, I like *boleros* (that's Spanish love songs). I actually like the new *boleros*, but I also like the oldies sometimes; it depends on my mood. Here in Los Angeles there are some stations that play music in both English and Spanish and where the DJs also speak in both English and Spanish, which is really cool, 'cause otherwise I'd have to keep switching back and forth between stations.

> I like—no, I love—to listen to the radio. I listen to it on the bus, in my room, in the car, everywhere.

I also like to watch TV. I watch the *novelas*—that's our version of soap operas. Ours end after six months though. How do you all watch a soap opera for 30 years anyway? We always get together for the last episode at somebody's house. Even my brothers watch them. That's about all I watch in Spanish, though. There's a couple of MTV-style shows I watch, but not much else. There aren't any shows in Spanish like there are in English, you know. There aren't shows like *Seinfeld* or *ER.* Mostly I watch shows like *Friends* or *Will & Grace.*

Do I like being Hispanic? Yes I do, but who thinks about it like that anyway? I am very proud of where I'm from and where my parents came from, but I don't dwell on it, you know. I speak Spanish and English, and I see it as a part of who I am, not something I try to do or think about. So when you talk to me as a Hispanic you better do it like a real Hispanic and not try to be all authentic with some really cheesy Hispanic stereotypes.

There's a difference you know, and I can feel it. I can feel when someone is talking to me as one Hispanic to another and when someone is using it as a ploy or a way to get me to like them better. When someone does that it actually kind of upsets me. I feel like they must think I'm stupid or something.

I'll tell you what I do like, though: I like when I see someone who doesn't speak that much Spanish making an effort to communicate with someone who does not speak English, and they are trying to do it in Spanish. I remember that, and I try to go back to that store or restaurant. When I see someone who is not Hispanic asking someone who is about the culture, about how to be proper and respectful, I like that too. When I get married and have kids I am definitely going to teach them Spanish and about our traditions, but I am also going to teach them the differences between being a Hispanic here and being back in Mexico or Guatemala.

I think it is going to be important I do that because right now there are a lot of us, but by the time I have kids there are going to be a lot more, and being Hispanic I think will be important.

Rodrigo Mendoza, Age 16, Orange County CA

What's up? I am Rodrigo Mendoza, but they call me Sleepy and I am 16. My parents are from El Salvador; they both work. I have one brother and one sister. They are both younger than I am. I go to high school, and I am in ninth grade 'cause I flunked a couple of times. I am a member of the Mara Salvatrucha. That's a Salvadorian gang that actually my dad was a part of. I've been to juvi three times for boosting cars and fighting.

I speak Spanish sometimes, but it's not like perfect Spanish, it's a mix. I speak it mostly with my parents at home. I work part time at this restaurant busing tables, and no, I don't know what I want to be when I grow up. I play soccer and hoops with my friends, but not on a real team, just at the school.

Yeah, I'm Hispanic, but so what, man? Everybody is Hispanic out here. No, I don't think about it fool, I just know I am. I listen to rap and hip-hop. I like Biggie Smalls and 50 Cent the most, but I guess Eminem's all right for a white boy. I don't like the blacks that live by where I live, and I think they don't like us. There's like a battle between us, know what I mean?

I watch MTV and shows like the *Wayans Brothers* on the WB. My homeys and I also read *Lowrider Magazine* 'cause we're into the low riders. Old school, you know. Now there's a lot of people that are into the Japanese cars that are all *mac'd* out with neon and super-fast engines and all that, but we like to kick it to something more mellow. Like I said, old school.

You know what I think is funny and actually kind of whack? When people try to sell you shit by making like they're all down and legit. I see all these ads and all these billboards that have like Spanish and English on them trying to sound like we do. It's stupid, you know what I mean, it looks stupid and it sounds stupid. How we talk is how we talk, you can't do it in writing, it looks stupid. I also think it's stupid how sometimes they be all like trying to use us being Hispanic to make us proud about it and shit. I ain't saying that other people might not get all proud, but for me and my friends it's just stupid.

Like the other day, we got this thing where they invited me

to talk about soda and candy and shit. They said they were going to give me $50 for doing it so I was down with that. They put me in this room with a table and 10 other dudes and then this guy starts talking about being Hispanic and language and how do you feel about being Hispanic and shit like that. I didn't say anything 'cause I wanted the $50, but I was thinking Who cares, man? I don't even really think about being Hispanic or if I'm proud or shit like that. Of all the things he showed, though, the coolest thing I saw was this commercial for a car. It wasn't a Hispanic commercial, it was an English commercial, but it had the Salvadorian flag in it. That was actually pretty cool.

Edgar Sáenz-Williams, Age 32, San Diego CA

Hello, how are you? My name is Edgar Sáenz-Williams, and I am 32 years old. You should immediately be able to tell I come from a different socioeconomic and educational background by the fact that I use two last names and by the fact that I used the word socioeconomic. I hope that didn't sound too pretentious, but it is the truth. I am originally from Mexico City, but my parents have a condo in Coronado that we have been coming to during the summer for as long as I can remember.

I am fluent in Spanish and English. That means I can write and read both perfectly. I have a bachelor's from the Technological Institute of Monterrey, one of Mexico's best universities, and an MBA from Thunderbird, one of the best graduate programs here in the U.S. I am now living in La Jolla, San Diego, permanently, running my father's interests here in the U.S. I am married and have three kids. My wife is Mexican and from a well-known family.

Since we have been coming to the U.S. for years and since we speak both English and Spanish, we really only watch English television programs. Most of the programming produced here in the U.S. in Spanish is crap, so when we watch Spanish-language television it is usually programming from Mexico. Mostly news and soccer games, although I love football and golf.

I have noticed in the past three years an increased interest in the Hispanic culture here in the U.S., obviously driven by the census numbers. I am also becoming interested in the Hispanic culture here in the U.S. After all, my children will grow up here, and I want them to maintain their cultural roots. This increased interest has actually raised my awareness even further regarding the sad state of Spanish-language media content in the U.S. I tune in to the television stations from Univision and Telemundo, and I come away shaking my head.

There is almost no newscast from any of these networks that provides a comprehensive look at world events. There is no interest in politics or the economy other than the interest in sensationalist stories that always seem to have a revolutionary or militant spin. I don't mean they should be dissertations on politics and economy, but why can't they look to improve the overall knowledge base of the population? Why do they always have to cover the story from the context of "The government is racist, and Hispanics get screwed again?"

Anyway, now you see why I try to not get too involved: I get upset, and I realize I can't do much about it. I will tell you that when I see a company sponsoring a higher level of program or event, like a good concert at the symphony or a golf tournament, I remember it. I also remember when I read or see or hear something advertised or marketed in Spanish that has been well thought out, that shows a true understanding of the culture.

Don't get me wrong, I know that I am not the typical Hispanic here in the U.S., but I am Hispanic. I also know that most companies are going to want to communicate with the largest constituency, which tends to be from a lower socioeconomic background, but what I can't understand is why they would try to capture or enthrall the U.S. Hispanic market by communicating with them at a level that reflects where they have come from rather than where they are going.

When most Hispanics left their countries of origin, they had hopes of a better life, of being considered as being in the same league as people like me. That's why they came here. It would seem to me that the most effective way to market to them would be precisely like that, by communicating with them in much the same way that you would communicate with me. Now that I am here for good you can bet I will try, in whatever way I can, to evolve our culture here in the U.S.

I want my children to feel like being Hispanic here in the U.S. does not mean that they have to make do with what's available when it comes to media, books, culture, anything. I can also tell you that I will remember those companies that speak to the best in us, not to the most common in us.

Jesús Olivares, Age 48, Houston TX

I am Jesús Olivares. I am 48, and I am from Honduras originally. I have been here in this country for 10 years. I own a small landscaping business and I have about five employees. I pay them in cash. I am married and I have two kids. They are 14 and 19, and they are both girls.

I speak mostly Spanish, although I have no problem communicating in English. I can't go into a lot of detail or be very flowery when I speak in English, but people understand me perfectly. My wife, Josefina, is from Mexico originally. She works part time at an office. She has been here for most of her life, so she speaks English perfectly, like my girls. Both of my girls are going to college, which makes me extremely proud since they are the first ones to do that from our family. Other than for work, I speak in Spanish all the time. It is still what I feel most comfortable speaking.

I watch Spanish television and listen to Spanish-language radio. On the radio I like to listen to banda music; that's like country music, but in Spanish. On television I like watching the news and soccer games and sometimes the Saturday variety shows. I also like the funny shows about hidden cameras and things like that. I watch that with my girls sometimes. I like it when we do that because I don't understand the music they listen to, that rap or rep or whatever—I don't understand everything, but I do hear the bad words sometimes. It is funny when they play the music and the singer says a bad word in English and they both turn to me to see what I'll do or if I understand it. I fake like I don't so I don't embarrass them, but I understand.

You know what kind of shows I love to watch the most, though? The shows about the pyramids or about the dinosaurs or about the history of Rome or Greece or other places. I only went to school until the sixth grade, so those shows help me learn about the world. All those shows are in English, but I can understand almost everything in them. When we go shopping I always pay attention to what my wife buys; she knows a lot about those things. Sometimes when I am driving around I look at the store windows, and when I see a sign in Spanish I like to stop and see what they have.

Néstor López, Age 34, Miami FL

I am Néstor López. I am 34, married with two kids. My family is Cuban and has been in the U.S. for 24 years. My father was a chemical engineer in Cuba, but when we got here he had to get a job as a building maintenance man. He worked for 10 years doing that, but eventually he started his own cleaning company. He has 65 employees now, and the company is still growing. My mom was always a housewife; my dad wouldn't have it any other way. I myself am a bank manager.

I speak Spanish and English perfectly, although I have a very hard time writing Spanish. My parents and their friends are very politically aware and active, but to be honest with you I just can't get as worked up as they do. Things back in Cuba are changing lately, and every time something happens there is a neighborhood reunion to talk about it.

I watch both English and Spanish television. I stick mostly to English because I think the programming in Spanish is very lacking. Even though I operate mostly in English I like receiving things in the mail in Spanish like coupons and offers. I like receiving them when they are well made and the Spanish is good. When I see something with poor Spanish and a dumb idea I do get upset. I am not big on claiming my culture and carrying the Hispanic flag. I am proud about being from Cuba and about what my parents have done, but to be honest there are a lot of stories like ours here in Miami.

I like when businesses try to communicate with me as a Hispanic because to me it is proof that we are growing as a culture and that corporate America is taking notice. That does make me feel proud. My family and I go to the Calle Ocho festival because it is the biggest event in Miami. It really has gotten big in the past few years. My parents and their friends never miss it.

I haven't told you about my wife yet. My wife is from San Francisco originally. Her family is from Switzerland, but she was born and raised here. What a mix, huh—Swiss and Cuban. It works, though. It is actually interesting because she acts more Hispanic than I do. She speaks fluent Spanish and reads all the

Hispanic papers. She loves cooking Cuban food and is constantly looking for the freshest foods.

Marissa Lozan, Age 27, Brooklyn NY

Hello papi, how are you? I'm Marissa, and I'm from Brooklyn, New York. I am from PR, that's Puerto Rico to you. Since I was born here but my parents are Puerto Rican I am what you would call New Yorkian. I have always lived here, but I go back to the island every chance I get. I am a hairdresser and not married yet. My friend Zoe and I are saving up to set up our own hair salon. I didn't go to college, but I know how to work hard, and I have taken some business courses like accounting and things like that. I am bilingual, of course, and I am a shining example of Caribbean beauty and "flava." I love listening to rap, salsa, and pop *baladas* (that's Spanish pop love songs).

What do I like to do on the weekends? Are you kidding? I love to go dancing, it's in my blood and I am damn good at it. I am very proud to be Hispanic, and I am very vocal about it. I have a Puerto Rican flag sewn into my backpack and a little necklace with the flag on it. I always go to the Puerto Rican Day parade even though it has gotten kind of nasty in the past couple of years. I watch television in both English and Spanish. I love the music shows on Telemundo and Univision. I also watch Don Francisco, even though he is kind of cheesy. I guess that's why my friends and I watch it: it's part of our culture. I also read *Latina* magazine along with all the other magazines like *People* and *Cosmopolitan*.

I am thrilled to death seeing all this attention the Hispanics are getting here in the U.S. It's about time! We are taking over, baby, and you all better pay attention, 'cause before you know it the majority of the population is going to be Hispanic. Well, probably not, but there are a lot of us. My mom lived here in New York until I was about 21. My dad left and she stayed here until I was 18, and then she went back to Puerto Rico to live with my aunt. The two of them come here about twice a year. I'd love to stay here and talk to you some more papi, but I gotta go, gotta go, gotta go to work.

Esteban Sánchez, Age 29, Fresno CA

My name is Esteban Sánchez. I am 29, and I live in Fresno, California. I have been in the U.S. only two months. My wife and son are still back in Oaxaca. That is a small town in Mexico. I am hoping to bring them here in the future. I speak no English, and I work in the fields picking strawberries. I live in a house with six other guys from Mexico. The work is long and hard, but this is what I came here for. I love this country, and I know that if you work hard you can make it big here; I've seen it. I was so surprised at how many Mexican people are here. Sometimes I walk around and everything is in Spanish, and it seems like I am still in Mexico. I do not know why it is, but things just seem better here in the U.S.

Since I do not speak any English, I watch and listen to nothing but Spanish radio and television. I cannot read very well, even in Spanish, so I really pay attention when I hear about things for sale where I live. I pay attention to the commercials to know what to buy. I listen to what they say, but I also really look at the package so I can get it when I go to the supermarket.

I go to a gas station after work to get a soda, and this lady is always there. She is American and does not speak a lot of Spanish, but she tries to talk to us anyway. She also has things from Mexico for sale that I love, like Gamesa cookies and spicy potato chips from Sabritas. I will always keep going to that gas station because I am always going to remember how nice that lady was to us even when we didn't speak English. I send about half of what I make back to Mexico, so things are pretty tight here, but my friends and I still have a good time on the weekends. We own one TV, and on the weekends we gather around to watch soccer or *Sábado Gigante,* which is a variety show.

Patrick Morada, Age 31, Chicago IL

I'm Pat Morada from Chicago, Illinois. I am from Puerto Rico originally. I've been in the U.S. for 18 years and I am a marketing executive at a Fortune 100 company. My parents are both from Puerto Rico. My dad is retired and my mom is a legal secretary. I have a sister that is going to college right now. I am fully bilingual and trying to learn French on the side. (I love cooking, and all the best books are in French.)

I am Hispanic and proud of it. More proud in the past few years, I have to say. I guess it's because of all the attention Hispanics seem to be getting lately. We are the largest minority and growing faster than any other group, so we represent a great opportunity to a lot of companies.

I have to say that I pay more attention now to the stuff I get in Spanish than I did before. I am always looking to see whether the Spanish is right or if it is a translation or if it even makes sense. It doesn't always, you know.

I listen to public radio and to a pop station. I watch the three big networks and HBO when I get the chance. I absolutely refuse to watch the crap they are airing on the big Spanish-language networks here in the U.S. If I am going to watch TV in Spanish I will watch CNN or FOX Sports in Spanish. There is some good programming coming in recently on the TV Azteca channel from

Mexico. What is really missing are Spanish-language publications comparable to *GQ* or *Details*.

I like to stick to what I know, so if I am going to try something new it has to really catch my attention, and—yes, I have to admit—good Spanish-language advertising and marketing does catch my attention. Advertising with a Hispanic element on mainstream television really catches my attention. When I was watching a show on ABC and a commercial came up in Spanish I actually stopped in my tracks. I am hoping more companies see the light and do more of that. It really makes me feel good about being American.

5

Spanish, English, or In-Between

O verall, the U.S. Hispanic population is divided roughly as follows: 52 percent prefer Spanish as their primary language, and 48 percent are bilingual or English preferred. I say approximately because various sources provide different answers.

We have taken a lot of these sources and come up with a median. Hispanics fall into two groups, those born in the U.S., not surprisingly called U.S.-born, and those born outside of the U.S., foreign-born. U.S.-born Hispanics are more likely to be bilingual or English-dominant or preferred. Foreign-born Hispanics are more likely to be Spanish-preferred or Spanish-dependent. Some people also define them as *Spanish-dominant.* Spanish-dominant or -preferred means the individual prefers to speak in Spanish, but can function in English if necessary. *Spanish-dependent* means the individual cannot function in English and must communicate in Spanish.

What is the importance of this in marketing to Hispanics? Well, if you already market or advertise in English, it is likely that you are reaching bilingual or English-preferred Hispanics, since their dominant language is English. If you are going to market or advertise to Hispanics in Spanish, you will most likely be reaching foreign-born Hispanics. And that means that you may be able to use information about their country of origin to be more effective when marketing to them.

I am going to concentrate on marketing and advertising in Spanish, because that is where most of your incremental customers will come from. The only exception to this will be Hispanic youth. We will cover Hispanic youth separately in Chapter 13 because they are a completely separate ball of wax. If you have done any marketing to Hispanics you most likely know that already. If you have never marketed to Hispanics, trust me: Hispanic youth are a market unto themselves.

Translation, Adaptation, and Original Creation

From a practical standpoint this is one of the most important sections of the book discussing the all-important differences between translation, adaptation, and original marketing or advertising development. The most common attempt to market to the U.S. Hispanic market is through the use of translations. This is as true of multinational corporations as it is of small businesses.

Believe it or not, many Fortune 500 companies that spend millions of dollars in marketing every year, use translations as the only form of advertising to U.S. Hispanic consumers. Now don't get me wrong. Translations do work sometimes. The operative word in that sentence is *sometimes*. More often than not, a direct, literal translation of English-language materials is completely ineffective, and may at times be offensive.

First, when you translate directly you have to consider that, generally speaking, Spanish is one-third longer than English. This means that if you are looking to print an ad in Spanish you have to make space concessions, as the length of your Spanish ad will be one-third longer than your English ad. Let's see an example. Here is a typical ad you would see in English and the translation in Spanish:

The Ultimate Sale!
This Weekend Only!

La venta más increíble!
Unicamente (Sólo) este fin de semana!

You can immediately see that the Spanish is longer. This is important when there is artwork that surrounds the content of the ad. When you translate you need to be ready to change the artwork to fit the Spanish content.

There are some other clear issues with direct translation of materials. When we come up with ideas for our ads, whether it is an ad in the local paper or a 30-second television commercial, we often use a turn-of-phrase, a euphemism, or any one of many other marketing elements that may have a double meaning and help to liven up the message. This type of marketing device is obviously not often translatable. There are some sayings that are the same in English and Spanish, but they are few.

What we need in instances in which we are using turns-of-phrase or common sayings is to adapt the ad into Spanish. I think the best way to differentiate between adaptation and translation is by saying that translations are about **words** and adaptations are about **ideas**.

Adaptation can be the most efficient and quickest way to get you started marketing to the U.S. Hispanic market. Adaptation in this instance is taking the main idea of what you are trying to communicate and coming up with its equivalent for the U.S. Hispanic culture. A true and effective adaptation takes not only the words, but also the tone and manner of the ad, and makes it work in the U.S. Hispanic market. To create an effective adaptation, you need to understand the cultural nuances of what you are saying in English and their equivalents in Spanish. This is critical to having your ad work as hard in Spanish as it does in English.

If you are wondering how the heck you are going to accomplish this when you are not Hispanic, do not fear. This is where having the help of an expert in the U.S. Hispanic marketplace will prove to be invaluable. Whether it is an agency or marketing firm or a single consultant, a good partner will help you to go through the materials you have in English and figure out whether you can just translate or you need to adapt. Depending on the level of involvement, your partner may also help to get you on your way if you need to develop something from scratch.

You may be thinking, "That's great, Maria from accounting speaks Spanish, we'll get her to do it!" No offense to Maria, but, trust me, it is a bad idea to do that—a very bad idea, with the potential to be a disaster. If you are going to translate your marketing communications, use the services of a professional translator. We will go over what to look for in a translator in the Getting Help section, Chapter 10. If you want to adapt your materials you will need to find a translator who is comfortable translating not only words, but ideas. This is not necessarily as easy as it may seem. Many translators have a hard time changing the words when they go from English to Spanish and vice versa; they are used to being very literal and precise.

6

Acculturation, Assimilation and Other Cool Buzzwords

I f you have already marketed to Hispanics in the U.S., you have no doubt heard one or all of these terms: Acculturation, assimilation, retro-acculturation, neo-acculturation, sub-neo-decaf-with-a-twist acculturation. . . . Get the picture? Let's deal with these terms now so we can get down to business.

Acculturation is a fluid process in which an individual picks up certain traits from a new culture, but maintains others from his native culture. Kind of like college: You are raised in your home town—say, somewhere in Idaho—with certain values, characteristics, and traits. You then go away to college—to, say, UC Berkeley—and begin to learn new values and customs and to acquire certain traits from your new culture. You might get dreadlocks or wear homemade tie-dyed clothing, but you will still maintain your basic traits from where you were raised. That process is acculturation.

Retro-acculturation would be when in your junior or senior year of college you decide you have had enough beads and folk songs. You begin to miss the culture you were raised in and want to go back to it.

Assimilation would be when you completely renounce your original culture and completely adopt the new culture. In our little example, it would mean that after college, instead of going back to Idaho, you actually stay in Berkeley, take up folk singing and go live in a commune.

Think of acculturation and retro-acculturation as a boomerang. It goes one way and then comes back to its origin. With that visual in mind, I developed what I hope will be a clear picture of the process of acculturation and retro-acculturation. The following graphics will provide you with a visual guide to the process that Hispanics undergo as they either get older or spend time in the United States.

The first graph will be for individuals born outside of the U.S., or foreign-born. Notice that the graph is based on time in the U.S. This means that the process of acculturation and retro-acculturation is based on the amount of time in the United States. Also, notice that the graphic is drawn on a scale. On one end of the scale there is country-of-origin influence. That means that the time in the U.S. reflected on that side of the scale is influenced by country of origin. And it makes sense. If you have just arrived in the U.S., where will most of your influences come from? The only place they can come from is your country of origin, of course.

As the graph shows, as people spend more and more time in the U.S., their cultural influence changes. As more and more time goes by, U.S. cultural influence plays a bigger and bigger role, until after about nine or ten years in the U.S., it exerts its strongest influence. I have also included in the graphic some examples of the types of initiatives that may be most effective with consumers at each particular stage of acculturation.

We then see the boomerang effect. We see that as even more time goes by, Hispanics tend to revert back to their country-of-origin influences. This is retro-acculturation for foreign-born Hispanics.

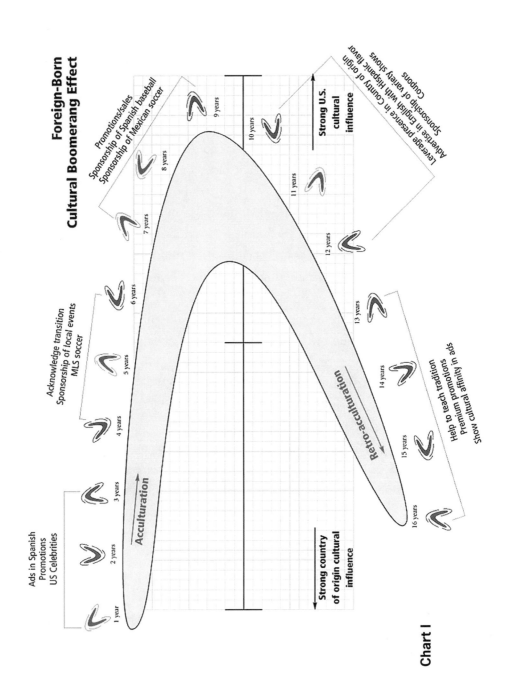

Foreign-Born
Cultural Boomerang Effect

Promotions/sales
Sponsorship of Spanish baseball
Sponsorship of Mexican soccer

Leverage presence in Country of origin
Advertise in English with Hispanic flavor
Sponsorship of variety shows
(Coupons)

Strong U.S.
cultural influence

Acknowledge transition
Sponsorship of local events
MLS soccer

Ads in Spanish
Promotions
US Celebrities

Help to teach tradition
Premium promotions in ads
Show cultural affinity in ads

Retro-acculturation

Acculturation

Strong country
of origin cultural
influence

1 year
2 years
3 years
4 years
5 years
6 years
7 years
8 years
9 years
10 years
11 years
12 years
13 years
14 years
15 years
16 years

Chart I

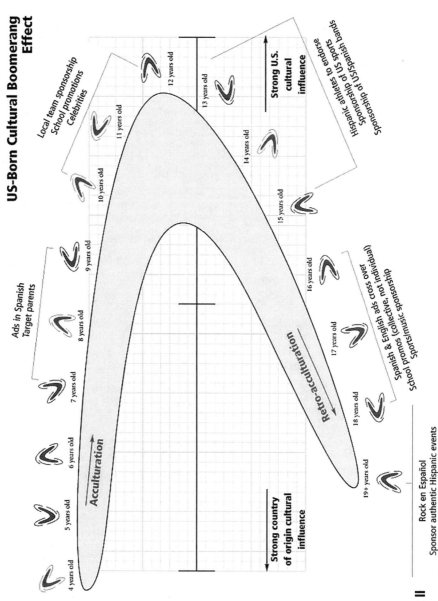

US-Born Cultural Boomerang Effect

Local team sponsorship
School promotions
Celebrities

Ads in Spanish
Target parents

Acculturation

Strong country of origin cultural influence

4 years old
5 years old
6 years old
7 years old
8 years old
9 years old
10 years old
11 years old
12 years old

13 years old
14 years old
15 years old
16 years old
17 years old
18 years old
19+ years old

Strong U.S. cultural influence

Hispanic athletes to endorse US sports
Sponsorship of US/Spanish bands
Sponsorship

Spanish & English ads cross over (collective, not individual)
School promos
Sports/music sponsorship

Retro-acculturation

Rock en Español
Sponsor authentic Hispanic events
Hispanic music groups crossover advertising

Chart II

The question you may be asking is, "What about U.S.-born Hispanics: how do they acculturate and retro-acculturate?" The answer is that the chart, as you have seen, is the same. The only difference between Chart I and Chart II is that Chart II is based on age rather than time in the United States.

What this means is that when kids are young—say under age 5—they are mostly influenced by their parents' country-of-origin values and customs. What our parents teach us is all they know and all we know as little kids. In Chart II, you can see that at a young age, children are in the process of acculturating, but definitely on the country-of-origin side of the scale. As they get older, they move into the U.S.-cultural-influence side of the scale. Then at about age 12, 13 or 14, U.S. culture exerts the strongest influence.

This is a period of time in which teens, being teens, are trying to figure out who they are. They are not sure they want to be Hispanics; they are not really sure what they want to be.

I went through this, as millions of other Hispanics have, I am sure. We changed our names from Juan to John and from Rafael to Ralph. We refused to acknowledge our heritage, and we refused to speak Spanish.

That dynamic has also changed in the past couple of years. Young Hispanics are now more than ever willing to embrace their cultures and traditions. The Hispanic boom in the U.S. has made it cool to be Hispanic.

In the past few paragraphs I have shared with you everything you need to know about acculturation for our purposes—our practical purposes. What use do we have for acculturation? When you are thinking about what part of the U.S. Hispanic market you want to sell to, acculturation is one of the things that will determine the language you do it in, the cultural cues you incorporate, and the type of promotional programs you use.

These graphs are by no means static. Depending on what part of the country you are talking about, the shape of the boomerang may change. On the East Coast, Hispanics tend to go through this process sooner than on the West Coast. This could be due to the countries they come from, the actual number of Hispanics that live there, or a number of other factors. Again, for our purposes this level of information should be more than sufficient.

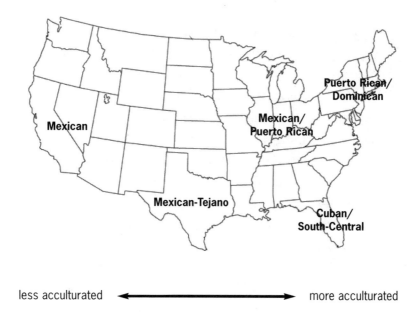

less acculturated ◄──────────► more acculturated

The map above should provide a good general guide. Texas is actually different than any of the other Hispanic markets in the U.S. in that, unlike any other market, Texas has developed its own blend of U.S. Hispanic culture: the Tejano culture. Many Texas Hispanics like to make the statement that "We didn't cross the border; the border crossed us."

All the Flavors

We know how the Hispanic population is divided by ethnicity, but how is it distributed across the United States? The previous map is a quick reference guide for how Hispanics are spread across the country. It is not meant to be a detailed map, but rather a way to give you a good idea of how things are. So now that we know what the market is composed of and where each of the ethnic constituencies generally falls let's get down to how each segment is generally defined.

Before all of you Mexicans and Puerto Ricans and Cubans and others write to me about how this is an incorrect description, let me tell you that it is only meant as a general idea of what we are all about. There is always an exception to the rule and yes, I know we are not all alike. Trust me, I have read some descriptions of our cultures in textbooks, and let me tell you, we sound like a pretty dry group of people. You know and I know that just isn't so, so this is my way to explain in general terms to our non-Hispanic friends what we are all about.

We Mexicans

Mexicans make up the vast majority of the U.S. Hispanic population. This is obviously due to the proximity of Mexico to the United States. Speaking generally, Mexicans are a very warm people. We enjoy company, and we are great hosts. We tend to be quieter and more deferent than our Cuban and Puerto Rican brothers and sisters. We do, however, have a fire that makes us very passionate when we need to be.

We are proud of our heritage, but are not too vocal or blatant about it. In recent years we have had to be more vocal, because many issues have come up in California and we feel there are certain negative feelings aimed at us.

On a lighter note, we love soccer and keep up with the Mexican soccer league. We like to buy brand-name products because we think they are more reliable and of better quality. We are mostly Roman-Catholic, although some of the other Christian religions are gaining prominence among us. There is also a vibrant Jewish community in Mexico, concentrated mostly in Mexico City.

For celebrations we have the obvious ones like Christmas and New Year's, but we also have some others. We have first communion and confirmation in our church. For each of these we usually have a big party. We also have a big party for baptisms. We take the job of being a child's baptism godparent very seriously. This is true of not only us, but of most other Hispanic groups. Our independence day is September 16th. On that day the president of Mexico comes out on the balcony of a very important building in Mexico and shouts, "Viva Mexico! Viva Mexico! Viva Mexico!" We then celebrate as Americans celebrate the 4th of July.

Besides birthdays, we also celebrate each person's saint's day (*dia de tu santo*). Each day of the year corresponds to a different saint, and on the day of the saint that has your name, you celebrate. For example, June 24th is the day of San Juan (Saint John), which means that on that day all people named Juan get to celebrate. We celebrate Halloween, although for us it also represents the Day of the Dead. We have little skulls made of sugar that we use to celebrate. We are learning to celebrate Thanksgiving, and we still take Easter a bit more seriously, although we are also learning to adopt some of the lighter and fun customs from Easter here in the U.S.

The capital of Mexico is Mexico City, or the Federal District (Distrito Federal), which is kind of like Washington, D.C. Most of the government offices and many headquarters for big companies are located in the capital. The majority of the population in Mexico resides in Mexico City, making it one of the most populated cities in the world.

We are very family-oriented, and we hold deep respect for our elders. We do not understand the concept of nursing homes. The only home is where the family is. We are very resourceful when we need to be. Even when we do not have a lot of money, we still get what our family wants, whether it is cable, a nice car, or electronics. You name it. We just make it happen.

We do have a sense of history, and we are very aware of the relationship between the U.S. and Mexico. We are constantly hoping that the situation in Mexico improves, and we talk about it often. Those of us who live here in the U.S., even the ones who just got here, love our country of origin, but we also think of the U.S. as our home, and we are willing to send our sons and daughters to defend it.

We Puerto Ricans

Most Puerto Ricans who live here in the U.S. are bilingual to some extent. We live mostly in New York, but constant access to the island of Puerto Rico helps us to keep our traditions fresh.

We are warm and gregarious people who love to have a good time. With a few sad exceptions, we are generally awesome dancers, and although we can dance to anything, we love to salsa. We are extremely social, and we are mostly run by our emotions. That doesn't mean we can't control ourselves, but it does mean we are effusive and impulsive at times when we interact with others. We can definitely be loud and argumentative, which gives the impression of toughness. We can be and sometimes are exaggerated, but that just adds to the flavor. It's not that we make things up, it's just that we add flavor to them.

We are passionate about our culture, and we tend to be vocal about it. One of the most explosive issues affecting us today is the question of whether we want Puerto Rico to become a full-blown state or remain a U.S. territory. We definitely feel a sense of community, and we feel like we are a part of a much larger group. Some of us are of African ancestry, so we actually have the best of both worlds: we are a part of both the African-American community and the Hispanic community. We love to make Puerto Rican food and enjoy when other people try it and like it. Puerto Rican food uses a lot of plantains and pork. Rice is a staple as it is in every other Hispanic culture.

Our language is Spanish, but it does have its twists. We call oranges *chinas*, instead of the more common *naranja*, and we call buses *gua gua*s, instead of the more accepted *autobus* or *camion*.

There are about 3 million of us on the island, and most of us live in San Juan. The crime rate in Puerto Rico is extremely high, as is the index of violent crime. Many of us are in the armed services, and it is a point of pride for us. Our undisputable pastime is baseball. We are proud of the fact that some of the best ballplayers in the major leagues right now are Puerto Rican. It has been like that for almost the entire modern era of baseball.

We Dominicans

We Dominicans are very similar in temperament to our Puerto Rican brothers and sisters. Our accents are almost identical. In fact we are almost the only ones who can tell the difference. We are also loud and gregarious and extremely social. We can be opinionated, although maybe not as political as Puerto Ricans.

Our sport is also baseball. Sammy Sosa is a national hero because of his accomplishments and because he still gives back to Dominicans. Our music is not salsa, it is *bachata*, which has a bit of a faster beat. We also have African ancestry in our culture. So even though there are many things that are similar between us and Puerto Ricans, there are distinct differences as well.

We Cubans

Do you have a question, because we sure have the answer! And we are more than willing to share it with you, whether you ask for it or not. We are very opinionated—we know it, and we like it. One thing is for sure: you will never have a dull conversation with a Cuban.

Like every other Caribbean culture, we are warm and friendly people with a lot of zest and a particular rhythm to which we march. Of all of the Hispanic groups in the U.S., we have the highest median income and we generally have the highest level of education. Many of us were already highly educated when we came over from Cuba. We were engineers, chemists, lawyers and doctors, and had to adjust to the need to get a job here outside of our realm of expertise.

Many of us who are middle-aged were a part of the political migration from the 1970s and 1980s and have established ourselves as a group to contend with in Miami. For the most part we tend to vote Republican since we appreciate the hard line Republicans have taken towards the Castro regime. And speaking of the Castro regime, we keep close track of what is happening back in Cuba since most of us still have some family that lives there. Although our numbers are small, we wield an incredible level of political influence. That influence used to be limited to Miami, but in recent years it has extended to the rest of Florida and the rest of the U.S.

Like other cuisines of the Caribbean, Cuban food uses a lot of plantains, pork, rice, and beans. Two of our most famous dishes are black beans and rice, and something called *ropa vieja* (old clothes), which is a dish of shredded beef in a tomato-based sauce.

8

¡But, I Don't Speak Spanish!

f you don't speak Spanish, it may be one of your first concerns as a small-business owner who would like to do more business with Hispanics. You might be thinking, "How in the world am I going to service these consumers if I can't speak their language?"

Let's analyze that. If you are selling a product, it is the product that is going to attract them and serve them, isn't it? What you want is for the consumers to buy that product. If you are selling a service, the first step is to get them through your door or to pick up the phone.

As we know, there are a number of excellent translation services that can translate your materials, and there are also many small companies that can adapt your ads to fit the market. Once you have the customers calling or coming through the door, it will be much easier to determine the best way to service them, whether that means hiring a bilingual employee, a freelance translation company or a phone interpreter service. The key is to get the customers coming in or buying the product first.

First, Show Respect

The truth of the matter is that the best way to sell any customer coming through your door is to show them respect and to provide them with the attention that they deserve. While language facilitates that, it is not the only way to do it and in fact is not even a prerequisite. Along those lines, I would argue that the use of the following five phrases would immediately engender a connection to any Hispanic consumer, and if you learned not another word of Spanish these five phrases could be sufficient to make your business a Hispanic-friendly business.

Buenos días/tardes/noches
Good morning/afternoon/evening

> Uttering these words when coming upon a potential customer at a store or restaurant, for example, immediately says, "I recognize your culture, and I would like to try to make you feel comfortable in my store." The Hispanic consumer comes away with the impression that this is a Hispanic-friendly place, somewhere he or she would enjoy returning to.

Cómo esta(s)? *or* Cómo le/te va?
How are you? *or* How is it going?

> Using this one will probably earn you a smile and a polite *"Bien gracias."* Sometimes it may earn you a string of words because it is immediately assumed you speak the language. In either case, you can benefit from this because you will once again be showing respect and understanding.

Cómo le/te ayudo?
How can I help you?

> This is a direct way of showing to your Hispanic customers that you are willing and able to help them even though you do not speak the language.

Que le/te vaya bien

> The actual translation of this phrase is "May things go well for you," but for practical purposes it is very similar to "Have a nice day." This is a casual and easy-going way to say goodbye and

at the same time make your shop inviting to your Hispanic customers.

Con mucho gusto *or* Mucho gusto

This phrase is like a two for one. *Con mucho gusto* means "With pleasure," and it is something you would say when you are asked for something or to do something. *Mucho gusto* means "It's a pleasure to meet you."

Notice that in some of these phrases there are two ways of saying something. That is because one way is formal and the other is informal. *Como le va?* is formal and *Como te va?* is informal, and similarly with the other phrases. Let's talk more about *tu vs. usted* because it is important.

Tu vs. *Usted*

In Spanish, as in many languages, there is a formal way of communicating and an informal way whereas in English, for example, the word "you" would be used regardless to whom you were speaking and regardless of the situation. In Spanish, that is not true.

In Spanish, the formal way of communicating is by using the word *usted*, and the informal way is by using the word *tú*. Without getting into a formal Spanish lesson, it is worth noting that once you decide to go with *usted*, all your communications need to follow that format. In other words, you could not use *usted* at the beginning of an ad and then switch to *tú*.

If you want to be absolutely safe, then use *usted* for everything. *Tú* is used when you are communicating with a young audience, say age 23 and under. *Usted* is used when communicating with an older consumer. You would also use *usted* when you are first introduced to someone. Likewise, *usted* would be used if you were marketing certain products and services, such as banking, finance and insurance. These products and services require that you engender trust and respect, and using the more formal *usted* is the best way of doing that.

Once you have gathered more data and can better determine the age of the consumers you are targeting through a retention or loyalty program or promotion, you may decide to be more familiar and informal.

Usted will ensure that you are not considered disrespectful or too familiar with consumers, which means that if you are planning direct mail it is the safest way to go. It is, however, not always the best way to go, particularly when you are selling to a younger consumer. The best approach is to determine the age of your primary customers and then use the most appropriate form. For instance, if you are offering financial services you would use *usted* in your first mailing. However, the response mechanism you provide should ask the question of how your customer would rather be addressed.

The Example of Jason Miller

Let's go through a practical example, shall we? Mr. Smith owns a small convenience store in Chicago. His store is in the middle of a Hispanic neighborhood, but he notices that a lot of people are walking past his store to shop at a store four blocks away. He wonders why. If we look at the outside of his store, we see nothing remarkable. He has all the normal point-of-sale materials set up in the window, and the place is clean; so what gives?

Now let's look at the store four blocks away. We see that this store has a large Hispanic clientele. The owner must be Hispanic, right? Wrong! The store four blocks away is owned by Jason Miller, an Anglo who doesn't speak a word of Spanish. So why the difference? If we look at the outside of Jason Miller's store, we can immediately see part of the reason. Outside his store, Jason has posted point-of-sale materials from Goya and Herdez, two well-known Hispanic brands. He has a couple of signs announcing specials on certain items in the store. Are his prices that much better? No, but the signs are in Spanish, which lets the people in the neighborhood know he is thinking about the things they like. When customers come into the store, they buy those products, but they also buy other things they need.

Jason fumbles through the transaction at the register, trying to manage with high-school Spanish, and although he butchers the language, his customers appreciate the effort. He has the greetings *Cómo está? Cómo está su familia?* ("How are you? How is your family?") and the phrases *Eso es todo?* ("Is that all?") and *Necesita ayuda?* (Do you need help?) down pat. Believe it or not, it is Jason's use of these phrases that has won his clientele over.

In this scenario, Mr. Smith can begin to attract consumers by following Jason's example. He can visit stores to see what Hispanic brands are carried and then talk to his distributor to get them in his store. He can also talk to the reps from the major brands he already carries—Kraft, Pepsi, Coke, etc. All of these brands target Hispanic consumers and will be happy to provide a retailer with point-of-sale materials in Spanish.

The biggest point I am trying to make here is that you do not have to be fluent in Spanish to market to Hispanic consumers. Put yourself in the situation. You are in a foreign country, and you do not speak the language. You go into a store and the person behind the counter does not speak English, but they come around to help you with a smile on their face. They take the time to try to understand what you need, and although you are not able to speak to each other you successfully complete the transaction. How do you feel about the whole thing: Do you feel taken care of? Do you feel good about shopping there? Would you come back? I rest my case.

It seems so insignificant that learning a few phrases in a language can make that much of a difference, but—believe me—they do. Learn from your customers. When they come in and you greet them in Spanish, listen to how they answer and learn what comes after that. You may not be fluent, but with each bit that you learn you will be deepening the relationship with your customers.

Here are some simple generic phrases that you can use on signage and point-of-sale materials in your efforts to reach Hispanics.

Gran Especial De Verano (Great summer sale)

Estamos a sus órdenes. (We're here to serve you.)

50% de descuento (50% off)

Compre uno y reciba el Segundo amitad de precio
(Buy one item get the 2nd at half price)

Lléveselo sin enganche (No money down)

Facilidades de pago (Easy payment plan)

Abierto de 9 a 10 (Open from 9 to 10)

Sólo este fin de semana (This weekend only)

Grandes Ofertas (Great discounts)

9

Where We Come From and How it Affects Our Outlook

One of the useful things to know about the Hispanic culture is something about the countries where we come from. It is not news to anyone in the U.S. that many Latin American countries are riddled with corruption and instability. That means that our threshold of trust is much lower than that of your average American when it comes to certain things. Let's look at the way some marketing methods, products, and services are affected by the places Hispanics have lived before they came to the U.S.

Coupons

A practical example of this is coupons. Most experts on the Hispanic marketplace will tell you that Hispanics do not respond to coupons, and they will point to study after study and to redemption averages to back up their claims. Some of them will also tell you that the reason Hispanics do not respond to coupons is because they don't work with or understand percentages. Well, they are only partially right.

The reason Hispanic consumers don't respond to coupons the same way general market consumers do is because they are not used to them. In most Latin American countries, coupons are not used. When they are, many stores do not honor them. That is one reason Hispanic consumers do not respond to coupons. Another reason is that coupons carry a certain social stigma for Hispanic consumers. While most consumers do not link use of coupons to socioeconomic level, some Hispanic consumers consider that only those in the middle-low to low socioeconomic scale use them.

Coupons can work when marketing to Hispanics, however. The trick is to know how and when to use them. A good example of a type of coupon that works with Hispanic consumers is a "Buy one, get one free" coupon (BOGO). BOGOs have extremely high redemption rates with Hispanic consumers, sometimes higher than at-large, general-market consumers. BOGOs are an example of the type of coupon Hispanics will respond to, but the other part of the equation is when.

> "Buy one, get one free" coupons have extremely high redemption rates with Hispanic consumers.

An example of the "when" is related to sampling. One of the most effective ways to get Hispanic consumers to try or change brands is sampling. This is actually true of all consumers; the reason it is so effective with Hispanic consumers, however, is word of mouth. Word of mouth is the best and most effective kind of marketing you can generate. There is nothing better than a Hispanic consumer telling his or her relatives and friends about a product or service. Word of mouth from those they trust is extremely effective.

What does that have to do with coupons? Let's say you wanted to sample one of your products, whatever the product might be, at one of the stores where your product is sold. Or maybe you own the store where the sampling is taking place. Either way, sampling is the best time to introduce coupons to Hispanic consumers. The most obvious way is to offer coupons for the product being sampled or for products that go with or can be used with those products. So, in the end, coupons can be effective to introduce new brands or products to these consumers.

Banking

Another consequence of the instability that many of us had to contend with in various Latin American countries is the precarious situations that banks many times found themselves in. In some Latin American countries economic instability often was the harbinger of the devaluation of the country's currency and the subsequent freezing of bank assets. Add to that incredibly high interest rates, difficult terms on loans, and a fluctuating rate of exchange, and you get a hearty "I don't think so!" when it comes to banking and credit.

Consequently, Hispanics who are recent arrivals are a cash-driven group. This reliance on cash can also be attributed to the many instances in which Hispanics do not have the necessary documentation to open a bank account. All these factors contribute to a lower number of Hispanics with credit cards and bank accounts.

As more banks turn their attention to capturing this consumer, that number will increase exponentially. In the meantime, many Hispanics currently pay their bills through money orders at check-cashing places. These places often offer a variety of services to address precisely this type of customer: check cashing, money wiring to their country of origin, phone-card sales, and payday loans are all financial products for consumers who live in a cash economy.

Eventually these people will move to more traditional banking structures. The key to being the leader in the banking arena will be understanding the evolution of the customer from check cashing and money-order buying to having a checking account at a bank. This understanding could be gained through partnerships with those companies that currently address the more recent arrival. Credit-card companies can also significantly increase their customer base of U.S. Hispanic consumers mainly by coming up with programs for the small business trying to tap into the market. Such programs must be based on more flexible requirements and alternative ways to provide secured credit cards.

Another possible product for Hispanics in the U.S. is the cash card.

Investment/Financial Advice

Investment and financial advice is a virtually untapped opportunity when it comes to the U.S. Hispanic market. The principal reason has been the perception that because U.S. Hispanics have a lower household income they have less disposable income and thus less money to invest. This is only partially true. Although there is a clear correlation between level of income and propensity to invest, it is not as significant as you would think.

Research among U.S. Hispanic consumers has indicated that one of the principal reasons for not investing or seeking financial advice is lack of information. It is kind of a Catch-22. The investment community won't market to Hispanics because they believe they won't invest, and Hispanics won't invest because they do not have sufficient information.

Now, once again I want to make sure that we understand that I am referring to the more unacculturated, Spanish-dominant U.S. Hispanic population. I am completely aware that there is a significant component of the population that not only invests but does so at very high levels. This more sophisticated Hispanic audience is currently being addressed and serviced on par with the mainstream population. The big opportunity for financial advisors and other investment professionals lies in tapping into that segment of the population that would like to invest and has the money to invest, even if it is at lower levels, but does not understand the process because of lack of information.

Health Care

Health care, like everything else, has some aspects that are just like the mainstream market and some aspects that are unique to Hispanics. For instance, Hispanics have a higher incidence of diabetes, but a lower incidence of diagnosis. So there are more diabetics, but fewer people who know they are diabetic. We also tend to be more likely to self-diagnose. If we don't diagnose it, our moms will eventually. And with mom's diagnosis comes a good home remedy for whatever ails you. If you are Hispanic you know what I am talking about. Chamomile tea bags to clean your eyes and heated honey and lemon for a sore throat are only a couple of the homemade medicines I had to endure.

One reason that we are more likely to self-diagnose is that in most Latin American countries you can walk into a pharmacy and buy whatever medicine you need without a prescription. This does not apply to narcotics and other "heavy" drugs, but if you need any antibiotic you can walk in and ask the pharmacist for what you need. You don't know what you need? Ask the pharmacist. Many pharmacists in Latin America actually diagnose and prescribe right there at the store!

Telemarketing

I think that the most important thing you need to know about telemarketing when it comes to the U.S. Hispanic market is the fact that it can be much more effective than it is for mainstream customers. Note that I said *can* be.

In order to be successful telemarketing to Hispanics, you need to ensure the quality of the Spanish in your scripts. Again, this is something a good translator can help you with.

The other and perhaps more important part is the quality of the operator. Unlike mainstream consumers who call to place an order, **inbound** telemarketing Hispanic customers are looking to get sold, not just place an order. They want to be greeted respectfully and they want to be engaged. This is where the operator can make all the difference.

When it comes to **outbound** telemarketing, the element of engaging conversation is even more important, and not only does the script need to be correct from a language standpoint, it also needs to weave in some elements of cultural awareness. Your telemarketing company should let you know whether it has the resources to address the main audiences: Mexican, Puerto Rican, Cuban and South/Central American.

What do I mean by that? Well, for example an awesome operator would be able to recognize the accent and adjust the script accordingly. If the operator recognized a Puerto Rican accent he might ask what part of the island someone is from. Or she might make mention of having a hard time buying *pasteles* (Puerto Rican tamales). This would immediately engage the customer and establish kinship and rapport.

Sports

If you have considered marketing to Hispanics in the U.S. you have undoubtedly been made aware of the Hispanic predilection for soccer, or *futbol* as we know it. It is true. Hispanics are crazy about soccer. Of course it also happens to be true of the majority of the population of Earth! Soccer is the most watched sport in the world bar none, and Hispanics are a vibrant part of that audience. But there is soccer, and there is soccer.

For most foreign-born, Hispanic soccer fans living in the U.S., the passion resides with their teams in their home countries. Regardless of how long they have been here, Hispanic soccer fans try to keep up with the standings, scores, and trades of the teams back home. So, an Argentine soccer fan would be able to tell you what place either Boca Juniors or River Plate is in, a Mexican soccer fan would be able to tell you when America is playing Guadalajara, and a Brazilian would be able to tell you what trades Santos has made in the past year. Notice that I said "foreign-born" at the beginning of the paragraph. That is because U.S.-born fans may not be as up to date. U.S.-born fans now have a home-grown league, the MLS, to root for.

So what does any of this have to do with marketing or selling to Hispanics? Glad you asked. These teams are big back in their home country, but here in the U.S. they may not even have an established presence, which means you can tap into them or their players for a much more reasonable fee than, say, the Denver Broncos. If you are Marty's Tire Emporium, using one of these players will garner you significant credibility for a fee you can actually afford. This is something that an agency should be able to help you with. The player, team, or league you select should match the makeup of the Hispanic population in the area where your business is located.

Now, while soccer is the most popular sport, it is by no means the only sport that Hispanics watch or play. Baseball is a strong second on that list. So strong, in fact, that if you look at any major-league roster you will most likely find that a significant part of the team is composed of Hispanic players. Most of these players come from Puerto Rico, Dominican Republic, Venezuela, and Cuba. Although there have been and still are a number of excellent Mexican players, baseball is most definitely a Caribbean-based sport.

Other sports that are strong among Hispanics are football, auto racing, and basketball. The NFL has been televised in Latin America for many years, although as you can probably imagine the football programming has traditionally been limited to the Cowboys, the Steelers, the Broncos, and the Raiders. Not surprisingly, these teams are among the best known and most popular among foreign-born U.S. Hispanics, regardless of where they live. More and more Hispanic players are making their presence felt in the NBA, and as the league continues to expand to include more international players, the Hispanic audience is sure to grow.

Again, what does this have to do with selling to them? A lot, actually. Just like you, the NBA is beginning to notice that the U.S. Hispanic population is growing, and like you it would like to better serve that population. Because of that you will find that many NBA and NFL teams are very receptive to advertisers wanting to communicate with the U.S. Hispanic market.

In summary, although soccer is clearly the most popular sport among U.S. Hispanics it is not the only sport that they gravitate to. Sports like hockey, basketball, and football may present some of the best value for your Hispanic marketing dollar.

Celebrities

Celebrities are an element of legitimacy for any advertising or marketing campaign. For less-acculturated Hispanics it is an even more significant element of legitimacy. This is because—unlike mainstream consumers—less-acculturated Hispanic consumers are somewhat less jaded. They haven't been marketed to as much, and so they are less likely to think, "This guy is just getting paid to do this so it's a bunch of crap."

For less-acculturated U.S. Hispanic consumers, hearing from a celebrity is almost the equivalent of word of mouth. For our purposes, what we need to keep in mind is that although there are a number of U.S.-based Hispanic celebrities, there are also some celebrities whose fame is significant in their country of origin, but who may not be as well known to the at-large U.S. population. Since we are talking about marketing to the U.S. Hispanic population and not the mainstream population, their value to an advertiser in the U.S. is significant. Their fees won't be. It is likely that a celebrity from a Mexican program would be much more accessible than a mainstream celebrity would be.

10

Getting Help

Finally, we have come to the point where we talk about getting help to do all this. This was a difficult section to write because I realize that many of the small businesses that would benefit from having a partner cannot afford one, and many of the largest corporations, having all the resources they need, do not choose to invest in the help they need.

In any case, I will try to make this section as useful to the small-business owner or manager as it will be to the major corporation. The most obvious and effective way to get help is to go out and hire an agency, a firm to help you put it all together. If you have the money to do so, it is a good investment. I'll go over that process a little later. If you do not have a big budget, we will try to come up with some useful alternatives that will match your budget.

Translators

The best first move is to hire a translator to take a look at your materials. Have him or her read what you have and give you a sense as to whether it will work in Spanish. You need to be careful to ensure that the translator provides you with an assessment not only of the language, but also of the ideas the language is trying to convey.

Pay attention to how the translator responds; is he or she confident in providing you options for the adaptations, or does he or she stick closely to the literal translation? You may want to get more than one opinion. Translators should not charge you just to provide you with a point of view on materials, or if they do, it should be a nominal amount. Some translators may outright refuse to do anything but straight translation, in which case you want to thank them and send them on their way.

There are many sources for translators, as a quick look at the yellow pages will show you. The quality of translations varies greatly, which is why I recommend that you use companies that employ only certified translators. Certification is a standardized test provided by an impartial organization to ensure the quality of the translations. There are two certifications for each language. You can get certified from source language to target language and vice versa. This means that a translator could be certified from English into Spanish, but not from Spanish into English. Make sure when you are looking for a translator that you ask about certification and who provided it.

The following two organizations are just a couple of resources I happen to trust, but there may be others in your area.

American Translators Association (ATA) is a nonprofit organization that administers the test both ways, from source to target and vice versa. They are tough in their grading, and their certification really does provide a level of comfort and confidence.

Translation Management Services is a Dallas-based company that specializes in procuring the best translator for each type of job. Whether it is medical, marketing, legal, or engineering, they will match the translator to the job. They use only ATA-certified translators.

Research

If you do not have the resources or maybe are not yet ready to hire a full-service advertising or marketing firm to help you in this endeavor, there are a few options.

Research in the Hispanic market has certainly come into its own. Started by a group of "daring" researchers three decades ago, the industry has evolved from simply tabulating Latino surnames to a wide slate of products that measure everything from brand preference to consumer attitude toward and usage of a particular product. Research is also slowly moving away from the tendency to segment Hispanics solely by language—Spanish-dominant, English-dominant or bilingual—towards more detailed segmentation.

Researchers now can segment the Hispanic population by such identifiers as place of birth, income, education, and level of acculturation. Evolution has been slow and steady, with dramatic changes coming only in the last three or four years. In addition to the obvious changes to the research itself, advertising agencies have jumped into the fray. They have helped to bring the message home to clients that finding out more about the Hispanic market is indispensable to driving their products' growth. Today, at least 33 Hispanic advertising agencies across the country boast market research on their slate of services. Some have hired a research director, while others have established dedicated research departments.

For many companies research is almost always the first step. They want to feel sure about their investment. For the small businessman this is cost prohibitive and, in all candor, of not much use. You own a chain of restaurants, and you want to know whether your efforts are working? Set up your own test! Take two of the restaurants and put your plan into action. Leave the third restaurant as the control by not deploying your plan. See what happens.

I bet just by walking into the restaurants you will be able to tell if something is working or if it isn't. If it does work, use it until it doesn't any longer, and then come up with something new. This kind of research is a fraction of the cost and can be twice as effective.

Obviously, if you own a larger business you will at some point need to do formal research. Whether you use secondary information like the census figures or commission custom primary studies, research will play a role in developing your plan.

Books and more books have been written on research. How to do it, when to do it, and who to do it with are all covered in these fine tomes. This book isn't one of them. What we do have, however, is what I hope will be a complete overview for those companies that are able and willing to commission their own Hispanic research study.

In my opinion, when it comes to the U.S. Hispanic market **qualitative** research is much more valuable than quantitative. I'll take it even further: **ethnographic** or **observational** research (research in which you go to the subjects where they shop and live instead of gathering them in a group and asking them to speak about something in front of strangers) is—bar none—the best kind of research. That is not to say that there is no value to quantifying ideas or hypotheses. It just means that if you want to get that nugget of information that will help you develop your marketing to the Hispanic culture, it is of more value to speak to consumers qualitatively.

The Hispanic culture is a passionate one, so it stands to reason that the most value would be gained by understanding the more emotional, human aspect that only qualitative investigation can provide. You, as the owner of manager of a store, can probably successfully execute an ethnographic study. You know the lay of the land: you know the regular customers, the traffic patterns, and the inventory. I bet with some input you could garner better information about your Hispanic consumers than any research company. That is obviously not the case with large multinational companies. For them it makes sense to hire a research firm, but the idea of the ethnography still holds true. It is the most effective way to obtain rich information about potential Hispanic consumers.

As you search for a company to do research for you, look for one that it is open to alternative methods of getting to the information. Make sure that it is open to providing you with a different type of report. You might ask if instead of a report, it could produce a video or a deck of cards containing key insights that can be distributed to employees.

When you are in the process of doing research among Hispanic consumers you will need to consider several issues that you do not have to think about when you conduct research among general-market consumers. This is true of both quantitative and qualitative research. The most important issue you will need to contend with is language. Who is it you want to do the research with? Remember that the Hispanic market is divided into English-speaking and Spanish-speaking segments, so it is not sufficient to decide you are doing research among Hispanic consumers.

If you decide that you want to address Spanish-speaking Hispanics, then you need to specify that to the research company, and you need to ensure that the moderator or researcher you work with is truly bilingual and culture neutral. This means that the moderator or researcher is able to conduct the research from a neutral perspective and will not skew it towards any specific constituency. Once you decide you want Spanish speakers you need to decide the level of acculturation you want your consumers to be.

Remember acculturation? How do you define the level of acculturation? Well, let's say you want to talk to less-acculturated consumers. The way to make sure that is what you get is to ensure that the following questions are included in the screening instrument:

- Length of time in the U.S. (the less time in the U.S., the less acculturated they are)

- Language they prefer to speak at home

- Language they prefer to speak outside the home

- Hours of Spanish-language television they watch per week

- Hours of Spanish-language radio they listen to per week

This series of questions will ensure that you are getting the right people for your study. You can decide what answers will qualify someone for your study. (When it comes to Spanish-language media consumption I would recommend that a minimum of 20 hours of combined television and radio be the standard for less-acculturated, Spanish-speaking consumers.)

Guerrilla Research

What about those smaller companies and businesses that cannot afford a formal research project? What do they do? Fear not, where there is a will there is a way. If you are in the retail business you can execute some research right in your store. Figure out what you want to ask, and then engage the services of a translator. Let him or her know what you are trying to accomplish and ask that the translator make sure the questions you have come up with make sense and will get you the information you need. You should also make sure that the questions you are posing are in no way offensive. Remember we are talking about a different culture that may find some questions too personal, even though they may seem natural to you.

Another way to execute qualitative or ethnographic research is by renting a Winnebago—yes, a Winnebago—and driving it to areas that have a significant Hispanic population. You can make up a sign asking people for 10 minutes of their time and maybe giving them an incentive to do it. A gift certificate or cash, anywhere between $10 and $15, should be sufficient. Once again, if you do not speak Spanish, engaging the services of a translator or interpreter will be crucial. Now, you have to remember that this person is not a researcher, he or she is a translator and will just be reading the questions and providing you with the responses then and there, so be prepared to take note. This technique can also be executed at a mall by just intercepting people as they wander around.

Remember the incentive, as it will be a significant inducement to getting people to work with you. If you have never undertaken an effort to communicate to the Hispanic market, any research you execute, guerilla or not, should prove to be incredibly useful. You will see the role language plays, the meaning of culture when it comes to what and how people buy, and you will also get ideas on how to best communicate with them as it relates to your own business.

Research Resources

This part of the research section is another instance in which I was able to bring in the insights of people who dedicate themselves to assessing companies addressing the U.S. Hispanic market, but who have nothing to sell to you and thus can provide a balanced and objective perspective. *Hispanic Market Weekly*, a Miami-based weekly newsletter published by Arturo Villar, was a significant contributor to the research section. *Hispanic Market Weekly* reports on trends in the U.S. Hispanic market, companies pursuing that market, and companies that specialize in providing services targeting that market. The insights this newsletter provides are extremely valuable.

The research products available vary in scope, size and cost. These range from custom projects created specifically for one client to syndicated studies that offer a general overview of the Hispanic market and are often available at reasonable prices.

Buoyed by the success of its Hispanic *MONITOR* consumer lifestyles study—and frustrated by the inability to compare results from the Latino survey and its African-American counterpart—Yankelovich decided in 2003 to do a comparative study that looks at Hispanics, African Americans, and non-Hispanic whites. The results are now available. See contact information in Appendix B. For 2003, the sample consisted of 3,600 people—1,200 from each ethnic group and divided equally among men and women aged 16 and over. There are plans to expand the sample to include Asians in 2004.

The two-step process involved recruitment of participants by random digit dialing, with the supplementing of Hispanics with a randomly selected surname sample. The first part consisted of 15-minute telephone interviews in Spanish or English, depending on the participant's preference. If the telephone was answered in Spanish the interviewer proceeded in Spanish, but if it was answered in English the respondent was asked what language he or she prefered to continue in. The second part could be answered by mail or via the internet in the same language as the telephone interview.

Custom Research Studies Created for One Client

In custom studies, the client establishes the premise that is to be analyzed. The methodology and questionnaire are then created by the research company. Custom research is generally divided into two categories:

- **Qualitative**. Gives insight into one issue, such as what consumers think about diapers. Through qualitative research, marketers try to understand what the consumer thinks about when considering a certain product. This requires in-depth investigation, talks with the consumer about what consideration goes into the buying process, and how he or she classifies the product. Qualitative studies are mostly done through open-ended questions with a moderately-sized sample. The general types of qualitative research are focus groups, minigroups and ethnographic studies.

- **Quantitative**. Provides statistical and quantifiable data about the target audience and its behavior. The sample is generally larger and the questions are close-ended, bound strictly by the choice of answers provided in the questionnaire. Traditionally, quantitative research doesn't explore the whys of the consumers' behavior. Some examples of quantitative studies are usage and attitude surveys, ad tracking and ad awareness, and opinion polls.

Syndicated Services

Several research companies conduct regular measurements of the Hispanic market, ranging from television and radio ratings to more general surveys of Latinos' product or service usage and preferences, and ad-tracking studies. These are released for public consumption at generally affordable prices and in some cases, highlights are posted on the company's website. Experts differ on their evaluations of these syndicated products.

- **Scarborough Hispanic Study**. A database of detailed demographics, consumer behavior, lifestyle activities, and media habits of the Hispanic population. The study concentrates on Hispanics in nine local markets: Chicago, Dallas, Fresno, Houston, New York, Phoenix, Sacramento, San Antonio, and San Francisco.

- **Simmons Hispanic Study.** Provides detailed information regarding what Hispanics view, listen to, and read, and their habits and preferences. Drawn from a sample of more than 10,000 Hispanics, the study represents adults in Spanish-dominant, English-dominant, and bilingual households. It measures demographics, attitudes, opinions, and interests, category and brand usage, ownership and purchase of goods, usage of services, and media exposure.

- **Nielsen Hispanic Television Services (NHTI and NHSI)**. Launched in 1992, the Hispanic services measure television viewing and Spanish-language television in the U.S. Nielsen

Hispanic Television Index (NHTI). It reports Hispanic audience measurement on a national basis using the People Meter—the same measurement tool used to report total U.S. audience behavior—with a separate sample of more than 800 Hispanic households. Nielsen Hispanic Station Index (NHSI) is a local service using a Spanish-language stratified sample to reflect the unique characteristics of each local market. The NHSI service provides viewing information in the top 16 Hispanic television markets.

- **Yankelovich/Cheskin Hispanic *MONITOR*.** Conducted every other year, this study reveals the social and cultural values and attitudes of the Hispanic consumer. The data, information, and analysis provided in Hispanic *MONITOR* is based on interviews with 1,200 Hispanic consumers aged 16 and older in 10 diverse Hispanic markets.

- **Claritas Market Audit Study.** Market Audit® is the largest syndicated database of consumer financial behavior. Compiled annually, the Hispanic subset consists of approximately 3,000 Hispanic households. The study measures use and balance information across dozens of deposit and loan products including checking, savings, CDs, IRAs, stocks, auto loans, student loans, and mortgages, among others. Channel behavior is also captured to measure online banking, use of ATMs, and more.

Testing

Testing analyzes advertising that is already running in the market. It provides a detailed picture of an ad's performance and effectiveness, whether on radio, on television, or in print.

Omnibus Services

An omnibus survey is a periodically conducted open survey that allows advertisers and marketers to purchase questions about a particular topic or product. Often many companies participate in submitting questions, but the responses become the exclusive domain of the questions' purchasers.

The omnibus survey has general demographic information that applies to the entire sample of consumers. In a typical omnibus survey, questions will cost $2,000 apiece, a considerable savings for the advertiser who would have to pay upwards of $25,000 for an individual study on its product or service.

Advertising/Marketing Firms

One of the advantages of addressing the U.S. Hispanic market is that since there is a fraction of the number of general-market, mainstream advertising and marketing agencies specializing in the U.S. Hispanic market, there is an agency or firm to fit even the most modest budget.

Even though Hispanic marketing has grown exponentially in the past five years, in my opinion it is still in its infancy. The Association of Hispanic Advertising Agencies (AHAA) is less than 10 years old, and the number of member agencies is still under 100. Even though it is still a relatively young organization, AHAA is the one of the best resources for finding an agency that is right for you. AHAA meets twice a year and at each meeting offers sessions to address the most current and pressing issues facing Hispanic marketing today.

Suffice it to say that AHAA will provide you with some excellent options. Member agencies cover the most significant Hispanic markets and some secondary markets as well, so you should be able to find a local partner or one close enough to satisfy your needs. Multicultural Marketing Resources is also a good source of information, although it is more of a directory. For more information, see Appendix B.

Because the Hispanic market is just now taking off as a significant business opportunity, there are fewer specialty firms to
address it. By that I mean that there are fewer PR, direct marketing, and interactive firms specializing in the U.S. Hispanic market.
For the most part these competencies are covered by full-service
advertising agencies. I am not saying that specialty firms do not
exist. They do. I am just letting you know that as there are a lot
fewer of them, you may need to engage a full-service ad agency to
execute on some of these efforts if that is what you are looking for.

Another type of burgeoning firm is the Hispanic media agency.
These agencies specialize in planning and buying U.S. Hispanic
media. Until recent years this was principally handled by the ad
agency. With the growth of the market and increased interest, however, a number of Hispanic media agencies independent of ad agencies have been launched. Although this book will provide the
small-business owner with what I hope to be sufficient information
to do your own Hispanic media planning and buying, larger firms
with more significant budgets would be foolhardy not to engage the
services of a Hispanic ad or media agency.

I would also like to note that if you have an ad agency of record
to address the general, mainstream market you should really think
twice about allowing them to do your Hispanic language media
planning and buying. Your current agency will almost certainly
offer to help with your Hispanic media efforts. Even though it may
be doing a brilliant job for you in the mainstream market it will
most likely not be equipped to do the best job for you in the Hispanic market. There are a number of considerations, language being
not the least of them, that your general market agency does not
have to contend with when it plans and buys your English-language
media. Don't get me wrong; your mainstream agency should be
very involved in the planning and buying of your Spanish-language
media, but only to ensure an efficient effort. Remember that there

are English-speaking Hispanics and that when you advertise in English you are reaching them. You want to plan and buy in order to complement your reach in the general market, not duplicate it. The following graphic will show you what I mean.

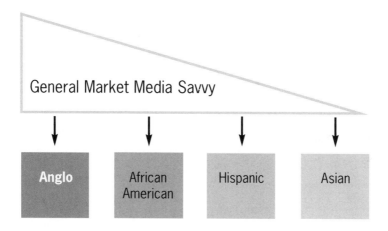

General Market Media

As you can see in the graphic, the level of understanding diminishes as we move from the mainstream, to the African-American, to the Hispanic, and finally to the Asian segment. The level of understanding reflects language proficiency and cultural relevance.

To explain further: Assuming that an ad was not developed using African-American insights or casting, a mainstream, English advertisement has the highest impact on the Anglo segment of the audience, as it is understood and processed. It has the next-highest impact on the African-American segment, as this segment of the population is English speaking and understands the ad. The impact diminishes, however, since culturally it does not incorporate any African-American insights. It has the next level of impact on the Hispanic audience and the least level of impact on the Asian audience.

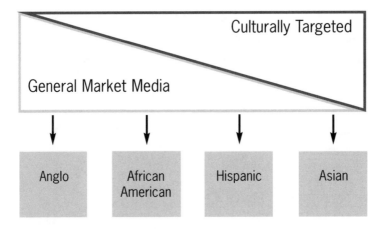

Remember, these last two segments have a significant component of non–English-speaking audience, so in addition to being not culturally relevant the ad is simply not understood. You can see, once again, that the ideal is to make sure that what you do with Spanish media complements what you are doing in the mainstream, English-speaking market.

11

Media Resources

We have now reached what is probably the most important chapter in this book. The right selection of the media you use and the way in which you use it will be the key to effective Hispanic marketing, regardless of the size of your business.

Let's get started with a few basics about the U.S. Hispanic media landscape and its differences from the general, mainstream market. One of the most obvious and significant differences is the number of options that exist to address the Hispanic audience compared with the number of options in the mainstream market.

Print

Think about the sheer number of magazines that you could possibly advertise in if you were addressing an English-speaking audience. I do not know the exact number, but it is in the thousands. You can basically find a magazine for almost any segment of people. There are gay magazines, gun magazines, surfing magazines, gardening magazines. The list seems endless. This means that depending on your business you could be very focused in your efforts. You can basically laser-target your audience.

That is not the case in the Hispanic market. There is only a fraction of the number of magazines available for you to advertise in. The circulation of these magazines is also not anywhere near what it is for their general-market counterparts. In fact, the magazines with the largest circulation are actually published by advertisers rather than publishing companies. *Avanzando* is published by Procter & Gamble, and Sears publishes *Lo Nuestro*. Both of these magazines are delivered and free of charge.

All of this may seem like a disadvantage, but it really isn't; in fact, I would argue that it is an opportunity. The cost to advertise in these magazines is substantially lower than the general market, so you get a much better return on your investment. Publishers are waking up to the need for more publications and are stepping up to the plate. There are many specialty magazines that are coming out with Spanish versions. These magazines are eager to establish an advertiser base and will be more than willing to work with you while they are building up their circulation.

Similar to the situation with magazines, there are fewer newspapers in which you can advertise at the local level. In fact, daily newspapers are available primarily in the principal markets we outlined at the beginning of the book. On an even more local level there are more and more newspapers, including weeklies, being launched in markets other than the tier 1 markets we outlined earlier.

Radio

One of the best values and most useful tools for marketing to Hispanic consumers is the radio. Besides the fact that Hispanics listen to the radio constantly throughout the day, the radio provides an opportunity to reach a high number of Spanish-speaking people with enough frequency to make an impact at the local level. Another benefit of using radio is that Spanish-language radio stations often organize events and promotions in which you can participate. They will even offer to help you develop an ad in Spanish. You can take them up on it as long as you have a second pair of eyes and ears to review it for you.

Another significant advantage of the radio is that you can be very specific about the Hispanic consumer you are targeting. You can define your consumer as more bilingual, less acculturated, younger, or older. Radio is most likely the best option for the small business owner looking to increase his or her customer base because it provides the best value for the dollar. If you do decide to pursue radio as an option you should keep in mind that when it comes to the Hispanic consumer you are better served by more frequency than more reach. You will be more successful running a commercial in non–prime-time slots for a longer period of time than by running it in the best time slot for a shorter period.

As I mentioned before, one of the best things about radio is the fact that when you buy radio you are sometimes able to tap into events that the radio station organizes. This is extremely useful because it allows you to develop a community-based relationship for your business. These events often take the shape of remotes, where the DJs actually broadcast from a variety of locations. You may be able to work with the station you select and organize one of these events at your own place of business. Hispanic advertising is still a relatively young proposition, and Hispanic radio stations are open to new and better ways to develop programs that smaller advertisers can buy into.

The formats in the Hispanic radio market are:

- **Talk radio.** Much like talk radio in the general market although fewer options for shows geared towards a specific audience such as investors, cigar aficionados, etc.

- **Banda.** This is music from the north of Mexico. It is akin to country music in the United States.

- **Tejano.** This music is very similar to banda music but has a bit more of an American taste to it. Although it is mostly in Spanish it can be bilingual, and it is specific to Texas.

- **Salsa/Bachata/Merengue.** Although this is Caribbean music from Puerto Rico and the Dominican Republic it is popular among all Hispanics. It has a tropical flavor that crosses all socio-economic and age segments.

- **Rock en Español.** This is exactly what it sounds like, rock in Spanish. This type of music has gained momentum in the past three years. Most stations that play this type of music also play Spanish pop or top-40 music. In some markets like Los Angeles there are radio stations that play it exclusively.

- **Pop Baladas.** This is basically top-40 music with a skew towards the romantic ballad. Like rock en Español, this format is often found in bilingual stations that play both English and Spanish music. As in the general market, this format has the broadest appeal from a consumer standpoint.

- **Sports Radio.** Sports radio in the U.S. Hispanic market is mostly driven by play-by-play broadcasts, although more and more sports talk shows are being produced. One of the most popular elements of Hispanic sports radio is coverage of the local soccer leagues from a variety of Latin American countries. The most comprehensive coverage is of the Mexican first division soccer league.

The two principal Hispanic radio networks in the U.S. are Hispanic Broadcasting Corporation and Radio Unica. Many of the stations that you will find in the lists I have provided in the next chapter are a part of one of these two networks. In the following chapter I have listed the phone numbers of some of the biggest stations within each market. This list will provide you with a general idea of what you could do in your market from a radio standpoint.

In summary, radio is one of the best media resources for the small- to medium-sized business and an excellent way for you to begin your Hispanic marketing initiative.

Outdoor Advertising

Another important advertising vehicle for the U.S. Hispanic market is outdoor advertising. Since the U.S. Hispanic population is generally concentrated within specific geographic boundaries, outdoor advertising can be an extremely effective medium. This form of advertising has expanded within the last few years to include some nontraditional formats such as shuttles, buses, and bus shelters.

There are certain considerations when you use outdoor advertising that are true regardless of the audience. Visual impact and simplicity of the message are among the most important. Among Hispanic consumers there are other considerations, however. When we say simplicity of message among Hispanic consumers, we are talking about making sure that the overall message of the ad is not too abstract or esoteric. Hispanic consumers tend to be a bit more literal and linear in their thinking. This obviously varies depending on the audience you are trying to reach.

Level of acculturation, dominant language, and age all influence the thinking of the consumer. Suffice it to say that more-acculturated, bilingual Hispanics are much like general-market consumers, but less-acculturated Hispanic consumers respond to a message that is direct and to the point.

Television

For a number of reasons, television is also an incredibly important medium with a lot of impact when it comes to the U.S. Hispanic market. To begin with, U.S. Hispanic consumers see an advertiser's presence on television as a sign of credibility. After all, the reasoning goes, they could not be on television unless they were serious and had the resources to do it. While for the general market, television presence does not necessarily mean that one advertiser is any more significant than another, in the Hispanic market it provides almost instant credibility. Another reason is that since some of the market, particularly at the lower end of the socioeconomic and acculturation scales, can be less literate, a clear visual component can be very important.

The biggest advantage of television advertising in the U.S. Hispanic market over the general market is that the small- and medium-sized business owner can actually afford to do it. Although the U.S. Hispanic television landscape has grown exponentially in the past few years, it is still far from what we have in the general market.

The biggest advantage of TV advertising in the U.S. Hispanic market over the general market is that small- and medium-sized businesses can actually afford it.

The marketplace is essentially composed of two principal networks, Univision and Telemundo. These two networks recently launched two subnetworks, Mun2 (Telemundo) and Telefutura (Univision), to address a younger audience.

Univision claims anywhere between 70 percent and 80 percent of the marketplace, while Telemundo claims the remaining 20 to 30 percent. This obviously means that when you are negotiating, Telemundo is generally more accommodating. For example, as a general rule, at the national level, Univision will not accept any advertising containing English: Not in the lyrics of the music, in the body of the commercial, or anywhere in the physical copy, if there is any. Telemundo can be more accommodating in this regard. In fact, a great deal of the programming for Mun2 from Telemundo is in English. In their desire to better establish their subnetworks and to increase advertising revenue in smaller U.S. Hispanic markets, both of these entities are aggressive in putting together packages for the small-business owner.

We should note that in some of the more significant U.S. Hispanic markets television costs are comparable to the general market when it comes to these two networks. Fear not, however; there are a number of smaller players that are making a strong entry into the marketplace. Among them are TV Azteca, Fox Sports en Español, and MTV Latino. These cable channels can and often do provide a better opportunity for the small-business owner to advertise at the local level.

All that being said, however, I should note that there is a minimum threshold of business that the television stations at the local level will adhere to. What that minimum threshold is will most likely depend on your power of persuasion and negotiation. Most channels have a minimum threshold of anywhere between 8 and 10 spots per week. For all practical purposes, any less than that would most likely not be worth your while.

When it comes to television advertising, one of the most important things you need to consider when negotiating your costs is ratings. Like any other media outlet, Hispanic television networks will provide you with rankings for their various television shows in order to explain why the commercial time costs what it does. This is no different than buying television time in the general market.

What is different, however, is the fact that when you are being told the rankings of these shows you need to have a clear understanding of which viewers those rankings are based on. For example, if I am network X and I tell you that 8 out of the top 10 shows watched by Hispanics are shows in my network I am obviously going to be able to charge you a premium for advertising on those shows.

What I might not tell you is that those rankings reflect only the Spanish-dependant audience within a certain age range. If I were to tell you what the top 10 shows were among all Hispanic consumers I might be forced to include shows like *The Simpsons, Friends,* and *Seinfeld.* The point is that you need to understand which segment of the U.S. Hispanic audience is really watching these shows in order to more intelligently negotiate your costs.

Internet and Email

As with the general market, the jury is still out on the value of the internet when it comes to the U.S. Hispanic market. Growing computer ownership and online access are two of the reasons that the internet is becoming a more valuable vehicle for communicating with Hispanic consumers.

Once again, the fact that Spanish-speaking Hispanics are concentrated within a specific group of users and the fact that there are not that many Spanish-language internet resources makes the internet a potentially efficient form of communication. However, as in the general market, you need to be wary of where your lists come from. If you are engaging in an email campaign, you want to make sure that the list is truly active and recent. I can't tell you how many clients have engaged in online efforts targeting Hispanic consumers only to find that the users they were targeting were in Latin America, or no longer at the address given, or English-speaking and not able to participate in the promotion or campaign. This occurs no matter to whom you market, but among Hispanics you have the additional factor of language to contend with.

If you want to make sure that you are dealing with a high quality resource you can tap into Yahoo! en Español, AOL Latino, and YupiMSN. These are some of the more established and well-defined portals in the Spanish internet universe. They are by no means the only ones; Batanga and Univision.com are also good resources, but the first three are in my opinion the way to go if you want more flexibility of audience and innovative online ideas.

12

Top 30 Markets

The following is a list of the top 30 Hispanic markets in the United States, based on population figures. The top 5 markets are obviously more expensive because they are what we would consider tier 1 markets. On the positive side, these markets have a wider range of resources that you can tap into if you are targeting the U.S. Hispanic population.

I think you will be pleasantly surprised at how easy it is to work with many of these resources. Many of them are young by general-market standards. They have been around 10 years or less. I only say this because they rely on people like you, advertisers, to come up with cool ideas to target their audience.

You will also find that many of these resources are more than willing to provide you with translation, production, and creative services. They do this because they want your business, and they want to be helpful and useful. They, however, are not translators or ad agencies, so if you choose to take them up on their offer, you need to know it is a hit-or-miss proposition. If you are a small business, I think you would be much better served to come up with some ideas of what you want and work with a professional translator to arrive at something meaningful.

You could also approach a Hispanic ad or marketing agency to help you with this one project. Some will tell you they are too large to take on a small project, but I think the majority will be willing to help you put something together. And if they don't, I will; so don't worry.

I have included what I think is the most important information you will need to make an informed decision, including population, market rank, and makeup of the population. (Remember that we are not all made the same—if you don't believe me, ask any of the folks I introduced you to earlier.) I have included the phone numbers for what I consider to be the main television and radio stations and the outdoor advertising companies in each of the markets. If the market you are in is not included in this list, fret not. If you contact any of the networks in a city close to the one you are in it will give you the number to their affiliate in that region.

Now remember, this is not the mainstream market, which means that if your town is small enough it may not have some of the same media resources as the other towns found in this list. There are still some cities in the United States that do not have a Spanish television station, for example. Suffice it to say that I do not believe that will last for long, as we see more and more Hispanics going to cities in the Midwest, Northeast and beyond.

This section contains some specialized terms for types of advertisements. Here are some definitions:

- **Super 30 sheet:** an outdoor board about 25 feet wide by 10 feet tall
- **Taillight display:** a board on the back of a cab or bus
- **8 sheet:** an outdoor board about 8 feet wide by 3 feet tall
- **30 sheet:** an outdoor board about 20 feet wide by 7 feet tall
- **Tail bus:** an ad on the rear of a bus.

You are now armed with enough information to access the Hispanic media resources necessary to launch your own campaign. As you move forward in this endeavor, you will almost certainly develop your own resources and ideas to address this market.

Los Angeles, CA

Total Hispanic Population:
6,845,339

Average Household Income:
$51,912

Hispanic Density:
41.3%

NATIONALITY:

Mexican	75%
Other	11%
Salvadorean	9%
Guatemalan	3%
Cuban	1%
Puerto Rican	1%

MAIN HISPANIC TV STATIONS:

Univisión 34 (310) 216-3434

Telefutura 46 (310) 410-8900

Telemundo 52 & 22
(818) 502-5700

Azteca América 54
(212) 207-8535

MAIN HISPANIC RADIO NETWORKS:

Hispanic Broadcasting Corp.
(818) 500-4500

Radio Unica (213) 337-2000

Clear Channel Communications
(909) 784-4210

Entravisión Communications
(213) 251-1011

Lazer Broadcasting
(909) 925-9000

MAIN HISPANIC NEWSPAPERS:

La Opinión (213) 896-2300

Mundo L.A. (818) 882-9200

El Salvador Día a Día
(213) 637-1980

Excélsior (714) 796-4300

OUT OF HOME:

8 sheets, 30 sheets, bulletins,
bus cards, full-wrap buses,
mobile billboards, taxi tops,
etc.

Clear Channel Outdoor
(602) 957-8116

New York, NY

Total Hispanic Population:
3,895,666

Average Household Income:
$48,399

Hispanic Density:
19.1%

NATIONALITY:

Puerto Rican	34%
Other	18%
Dominican	13%
Ecuadorian	12%
Colombian	10%
Mexican	9%
Cuban	4%

MAIN HISPANIC TV STATIONS:

Univision 41 (201) 287-4141

Telefutura 68 (201) 287-4141

Telemundo 47 (212) 492-5500

MAIN HISPANIC RADIO NETWORKS:

Hispanic Broadcasting Corp.
(212) 310-6000

Radio Cumbre (203) 335-1450

Multicultural Broadcasting
(212) 966-1059

Spanish Broadcasting System
(212) 541-9200

MAIN HISPANIC NEWSPAPERS:

La Prensa (212) 807-4679

Hoy (212) 290-9292

Noticias del Mundo
(718) 786-4343

La Voz Hispana
(212) 348-8270

OUT OF HOME:

8 sheets, 30 sheets, bulletins,
bus cards, full-wrap buses,
mobile billboards, taxi tops,
phone kiosks, subway 2
sheets, subway cards, transit
shelters, etc.

Clear Channel Outdoor
(602) 957-8116

Zoom Media (212) 685-7981

Massive Media
(212) 730-7222

Icono Media (888) 584-6279

Miami–Fort Lauderdale, FL

Total Hispanic Population:
1,652,165

Average Household Income:
$57,472

Hispanic Density:
40.7%

NATIONALITY:

Cuban	45%
Other	21%
Colombian	12%
Puerto Rican	9%
Hondurian	5%
Nicaraguan	4%
Mexican	4%

MAIN HISPANIC TV STATIONS:

Univision 23 (305) 471-3900

Telefutura 69 (305) 471-3900

Telemundo 51 (305) 888-5151

MAIN HISPANIC RADIO NETWORKS:

Hispanic Broadcasting Corp.
(305) 447-1140

Radio Unica (305) 463-5000

Spanish Broadcasting System
(305) 444-9292

South Broadcasting Systems
(305) 529-0006

MAIN HISPANIC NEWSPAPERS:

Diario Las Americas
(305) 633-3341

El Nuevo Herald
(305) 376-8919

El Sentinel (954) 356-4553

OUT OF HOME:

8 sheets, 30 sheets, bulletins, bus cards, full-wrap buses, mobile billboards, taxi tops, mall dioramas, phone kiosks, airport shuttles, lunch trucks, super 30 sheets, transit shelters, taillight displays, etc.

AdsOnPhones (301) 770-1122

Zoom Media (212) 685-7981

Icono Media (888) 584-6279

Chicago, IL

Total Hispanic Population:
1,587,360

Average Household Income:
$52,303

Hispanic Density:
16.9%

NATIONALITY:

Mexican	75%
Puerto Rican	11%
Other	7%
Guatemalan	4%
Salvadorean	2%
Cuban	1%

MAIN HISPANIC TV STATIONS:

Univision 66 (312) 670-1000
Telefutura 60 (312) 467-9000
Telemundo 44 (773) 244-7140

MAIN HISPANIC RADIO NETWORKS:

Hispanic Broadcasting Corp.
(312) 751-5560

Radio Unica (312) 279-9100

Spanish Broadcasting System
(312) 920-9500

Entravision Communications
(773) 767-1000

MAIN HISPANIC NEWSPAPERS:

La Raza (773) 273-2900
La Voz (773) 221-9416
El Día (708) 652-5397

OUT OF HOME:

8 sheets, 30 sheets, bulletins, bus cards, full-wrap buses, mobile billboards, taxi tops, mall dioramas, transit shelters, etc.

AdsOnPhones (301) 770-1122

Zoom Media (212) 685-7981

Icono Media (888) 584-6279

Clear Channel Outdoor
(602) 957-8116

5 Houston, TX

Total Hispanic Population:
1,526,137

Average Household Income:
$46,094

Hispanic Density:
29.3%

NATIONALITY:

Mexican	73%
Salvadorean	9%
Other	7%
Colombian	4%
Guatemalan	3%
Cuban	1%
Puerto Rican	1%

MAIN HISPANIC TV STATIONS:

Univision 45 (713) 662-4545
Telefutura 67 (713) 662-4545
Telemundo 48 (713) 974-4848

MAIN HISPANIC RADIO NETWORKS:

Hispanic Broadcasting Corp.
(713) 4
Radio Unica (713) 334-1320
Liberman Broadcasting
(281) 493-2900

MAIN HISPANIC NEWSPAPERS:

La Voz de Houston
(713) 644-7449
Semana (713) 774-4683
El Mexicano (713) 674-5501

OUT OF HOME:

8 sheets, 30 sheets, bulletins, mall dioramas, mobile bill-boards,lunch trucks, etc.

AdsOnPhones (301) 770-1122
Zoom Media (212) 685-7981
Icono Media (888) 584-6279
Clear Channel Outdoor
(602) 957-8116

6   San Francisco–Oakland–San Jose, CA

Total Hispanic Population:
1,367,703
Average Household Income:
$46,094
Hispanic Density:
19.9%

NATIONALITY:

Mexican	70%
Other	12%
Salvadorean	9%
Hondurian	3%
Guatemalan 3%	
Puerto Rican	2%
Cuban	1%

MAIN HISPANIC TV STATIONS:

Univision 14 (415) 538-8000
Telefutura 66 (415) 538-6466
Telemundo 52 (408) 435-8848

MAIN HISPANIC RADIO NETWORKS:

Hispanic Broadcasting Corp.
(415) 989-5765
Radio Unica (415) 695-1010
Entravision Communications
(408) 540-5683

MAIN HISPANIC NEWSPAPERS:

El Bohemio (415) 469-9579
El Mensajero (415) 206-7230
El Observador (408) 938-1700
El Mundo (510) 763-1120
Nuevo Mundo (888) 777-8711

OUT OF HOME:

8 sheets, 30 sheets, bulletins,
mall dioramas, mobile bill-
boards, lunch trucks, etc.
AdsOnPhones (301) 770-1122
Zoom Media (212) 685-7981
Icono Media (888) 584-6279
Clear Channel Outdoor
(602) 957-8116

7 Dallas-Fort Worth, TX

Total Hispanic Population:
1,287,752

Average Household Income:
$42,735

Hispanic Density:
21.4%

NATIONALITY:

Mexican	79%
Other	14%
Salvadorean	5%
Puerto Rican	1%
Cuban	1%

MAIN HISPANIC TV STATIONS:

Univision 23 (214) 758-2300
Telefutura 49 (214) 954-4900
Telemundo 39 (214) 523-3900

MAIN HISPANIC RADIO NETWORKS:

Hispanic Broadcasting Corp.
(214) 525-0400
Radio Unica (214) 599-9788
Entravision Communications
(214) 841-4689

MAIN HISPANIC NEWSPAPERS:

El Extra (214) 309-0990
El Líder USA (214) 942-4580
El Heraldo News
(214) 827-9700
La Subasta (214) 951-9500

OUT OF HOME:

8 sheets, 30 sheets, bulletins, mobile billboards, lunch trucks, buses, full-wrap buses, etc.
AdsOnPhones (301) 770-1122
Zoom Media (212) 685-7981
Icono Media (888) 584-6279
Clear Channel Outdoor
(602) 957-8116

8   San Antonio, TX

Total Hispanic Population:
  1,075,603

Average Household Income:
  $37,077

Hispanic Density:
  52%

NATIONALITY:

Mexican	71%
Other	27%
Puerto Rican	1%
Cuban	1%

MAIN HISPANIC TV STATIONS:

Univision 41 (210) 227-4141

Telefutura 17 (210) 227-4141

Telemundo 60 (210) 340-8860

MAIN HISPANIC RADIO NETWORKS:

Hispanic Broadcasting Corp.
  (210) 829-1075

Radio Unica (210) 280-4000

Spanish Broadcasting System
  (210) 340-1234

MAIN HISPANIC NEWSPAPERS:

Express-News (210) 250-2503

La Prensa de San Antonio
  (210) 242-7900

La Prensita (210) 242-7900

OUT OF HOME:

8 sheets, 30 sheets, bulletins, mobile billboards, lunch trucks, tail buses, full-wrap buses, etc.

AdsOnPhones (301) 770-1122

Icono Media (888) 584-6279

Clear Channel Outdoor
  (602) 957-8116

 **Phoenix, AZ**

Total Hispanic Population:
990,571

Average Household Income:
$41,123

Hispanic Density:
23.9%

NATIONALITY:

Mexican	81%
Other	17%
Puerto Rican	1%
Cuban	1%

MAIN HISPANIC TV STATIONS:

Univision 33 (602) 243-3333

Telefutura 13 (928) 527-1300

Telemundo 48 (602) 268-2648

MAIN HISPANIC RADIO NETWORKS:

Hispanic Broadcasting Corp.
(602) 308-7900

Radio Unica (602) 234-8998

Entravision Communications
(602) 266-2005

MAIN HISPANIC NEWSPAPERS:

La Voz (602) 253-9080

Prensa Hispana
(602) 256-2443

OUT OF HOME:

8 sheets, 30 sheets, bulletins, mobile billboards, lunch trucks, tail buses, full-wrap buses, etc.

AdsOnPhones (301) 770-1122

Icono Media (888) 584-6279

Clear Channel Outdoor
(602) 957-8116

Zoom Media (212) 685-7981

10 Harlingen–Weslaco–Brownsville–McAllen, TX (Rio Grande Valley)

Total Hispanic Population:
903,256

Average Household Income:
$40,114

Hispanic Density:
87%

NATIONALITY:

Mexican	90%
Other	8%
Puerto Rican	1%
Cuban	1%

MAIN HISPANIC TV STATIONS:

Univision 48 (956) 687-4848

Telemundo 40 (602) 268-2648

Televisa 7
(011-52-88) 17-7270

in Mexico
Liberty 4 (956) 421-4444

MAIN HISPANIC RADIO NETWORKS:

Hispanic Broadcasting Corp.
(956) 631-5499

Radio Unica (956) 668-8585

Entravision Communications
(956) 661-6000

MAIN HISPANIC NEWSPAPERS:

El Clamor (956) 994-3996

El Periodico USA
(956) 631-5628

OUT OF HOME:

8 sheets, 30 sheets, bulletins, mobile billboards, lunch truck.

AdsOnPhones (301) 770-1122

Icono Media (888) 584-6279

Lamar Advertising
(361) 299-5550

Fresno–Visalia, CA

Total Hispanic Population:
801,357

Average Household Income:
$43,321

Hispanic Density:
46.7%

NATIONALITY:

Mexican	86%
Other	14%

MAIN HISPANIC TV STATIONS:

Univision 21 & 41
(559) 222-2121

Telefutura 61 (559) 255-1161

Caballero 16 & 7
(972) 503-6800

MAIN HISPANIC RADIO NETWORKS:

Entravision Communications
(559) 455-0180

Lotus Communications
(559) 497-1100

MAIN HISPANIC NEWSPAPERS:

Vida en el Valle
(559) 441-6780

OUT OF HOME:

8 sheets, 30 sheets, bulletins, mobile billboards, lunch trucks, full-wrap buses, etc.

AdsOnPhones (301) 770-1122

Icono Media (888) 584-6279

Vista Media/Fresno
(559) 233-5828

Clear Channel Outdoor
(602) 957-8116

Targeted Access Media
(212) 268-8388

San Diego, CA

Total Hispanic Population:
798,988

Average Household Income:
$45,001

Hispanic Density:
27.6%

NATIONALITY:

Mexican	84%
Other	16%

MAIN HISPANIC TV STATIONS:

Univision 17 (858) 576-1919

Televisa 45 (619) 230-0203

Televisa 12 (619) 585-9398

Televisa 23 (619) 585-9398

MAIN HISPANIC RADIO NETWORKS:

Hispanic Broadcasting Corp.
(619) 235-0600

Clear Channel Communications
(858) 292-2000

Cadena Baja California
(619) 230-0203

MAIN HISPANIC NEWSPAPERS:

El Mexicano (619) 267-6010

El Latino San Diego
(619) 426-1491

La Prensa San Diego
(619) 231-2873

Hispanos Unidos
(760) 740-9561

OUT OF HOME:

8 sheets, 30 sheets, bulletins,
mobile billboards, lunch trucks,
Full tail buses, full-wrap buses,
taxi tops, transit shelters, etc.

AdsOnPhones (301) 770-1122

Icono Media (888) 584-6279

Clear Channel Outdoor
(602) 957-8116

Trykor Mobile Marketing
(760) 726-9498

Sacramento–Stockton–Modesto, CA

Total Hispanic Population:
735,625

Average Household Income:
$43,495

Hispanic Density:
20.9%

NATIONALITY:

Mexican	91%
Other	9%

MAIN HISPANIC TV STATIONS:

Univision 19 (916) 927-1900

Telefutura 27 (916) 927-1900

Caballero 14, 47 & 15
(972) 503-6800

MAIN HISPANIC RADIO NETWORKS:

Entravision Communications
(209) 474-0154

MAIN HISPANIC NEWSPAPERS:

El Hispano (916) 442-0267

OUT OF HOME:

8 sheets, 30 sheets, bulletins, mobile billboards, lunch trucks, full-wrap buses, transit shelters, etc.

AdsOnPhones (301) 770-1122

Icono Media (888) 584-6279

Clear Channel Outdoor
(602) 957-8116

Targeted Access Media
(212) 268-8388

Jacobs Billboard
(916) 646-6665

El Paso, TX

Total Hispanic Population:
670,646

Average Household Income:
$38,189

Hispanic Density:
76.3%

NATIONALITY:

Mexican   82%

Other   18%

MAIN HISPANIC TV STATIONS:

Univision 26 (N/A)

Telemundo 48 (N/A)

Entravision 65
(915) 581-1126

Televisa 2, 32 & 56
(956) 972-0476

MAIN HISPANIC RADIO NETWORKS:

Hispanic Broadcasting Corp.
(915) 565-2999

Organizacion Radio Centro
(915) 542-2969

Entravision Communications
(915) 581-1126

MAIN HISPANIC NEWSPAPERS:

El Paso Times
(915) 546-6237

OUT OF HOME:

8 sheets, 30 sheets, bulletins,
mobile billboards, taxi tops.

AdsOnPhones (301) 770-1122

Icono Media (888) 584-6279

Clear Channel Outdoor
(602) 957-8116

Targeted Access Media
(212) 268-8388

El Paso Southwest Outdoor
(915) 533-2265

Albuquerque–Santa Fe, NM

Total Hispanic Population:
650,988

Average Household Income:
$35,733

Hispanic Density:
38.1%

NATIONALITY:

Mexican	66%
Other	34%

MAIN HISPANIC TV STATIONS:

Univision 41 (505) 342-4141

Telefutura 48 (505) 342-4141

MAIN HISPANIC RADIO NETWORKS:

Hispanic Broadcasting Corp.
(505) 262-1142

Runnels Broadcasting System
(505) 622-0290

Entravision Communications
(505) 342-4141

Clear Channel Communications
(505) 830-6400

MAIN HISPANIC NEWSPAPERS:

Santa Fe New Mexican
(505) 983-3303

El Hispano News
(505) 243-6161

Santa Fe Reporter
(505) 988-5541

OUT OF HOME:

8 sheets, 30 sheets, bulletins,
mobile billboards.
AdsOnPhones
(301) 770-1122

Icono Media (888) 584-6279

Clear Channel Outdoor
(602) 957-8116

Denver, CO

Total Hispanic Population:
627,556
Average Household Income:
$39,291
Hispanic Density:
17.6%

NATIONALITY:

Mexican   66%
Other   34%

MAIN HISPANIC TV STATIONS:
Univision 50 (303) 832-0050
Telefutura 43 (303) 832-0050
Telemundo 63 (303) 832-0402

MAIN HISPANIC RADIO NETWORKS:
Entravision Communications
(303) 721-9210

MAIN HISPANIC NEWSPAPERS:
El Hispano (303) 340-0303
La Voz (303) 936-8556

OUT OF HOME:
8 sheets, 30 sheets, bulletins,
mobile billboards, transit
shelters
AdsOnPhones (301) 770-1122
Icono Media (888) 584-6279
Targeted Access Media
(212) 268-8388

Philadelphia, PA

Total Hispanic Population:
  502,967
Average Household Income:
  $38,375
Hispanic Density:
  6.6%

NATIONALITY:
  Puerto Rican 59%
  Other   28%
  Mexican   13%

MAIN HISPANIC TV STATIONS:
  Univision 65 (856) 691-6565
  Telefutura 28 (215) 568-2800

MAIN HISPANIC RADIO NETWORKS:
  Mega Communications
    (215) 426-1900

MAIN HISPANIC NEWSPAPERS:
  Al Día (215) 569-4666
  El Hispano (610) 789-5512
  El Sol Latino (215) 424-1200
  Unidad Latina (610) 932-2444

OUT OF HOME:
  8 sheets, 30 sheets, bulletins,
  mobile billboards, transit
  shelters
  AdsOnPhones (301) 770-1122
  Icono Media (888) 584-6279
  Targeted Access Media
    (212) 268-8388
  Clear Channel Outdoor
    (602) 957-8116
  Zoom Media (212) 685-7981
  Nextmedia Outdoor
    (908) 810-9901

Washington, DC

Total Hispanic Population:
  483,563
Average Household Income:
  $45,563
Hispanic Density:
  8.4%

NATIONALITY:
  Other   77%
  Mexican   16%
  Puerto Rican   7%

MAIN HISPANIC TV STATIONS:
  Univision 30 (301) 589-0030
  Telefutura 14 (301) 589-0030
  Telemundo 64 (703) 820-8333

MAIN HISPANIC RADIO NETWORKS:
  Mega Communications
    (301) 588-6200

MAIN HISPANIC NEWSPAPERS:
  El Tiempo Latino
    (703) 527-7860
  El Pregonero (202) 281-2440
  Washington Hispanic
    (202) 667-8881

OUT OF HOME:
  8 sheets, 30 sheets, bulletins, mobile billboards, transit shelters, bus shelters, taxis, buses
  AdsOnPhones (301) 770-1122
  Icono Media (888) 584-6279
  Clear Channel Outdoor
    (602) 957-8116
  Zoom Media (212) 685-7981

Tampa–ST. Petersburg–Sarasota, FL

Total Hispanic Population:
393,204

Average Household Income:
$41,856

Hispanic Density:
10.2%

NATIONALITY:

Mexican	32%
Other	28%
Puerto Rican	27%
Cuban	13%

MAIN HISPANIC TV STATIONS:

Univision 62 (813) 872-6262

Telefutura 50 (813) 684-5550

Telemundo 49 (813) 319-5757

MAIN HISPANIC RADIO NETWORKS:

Mega Communications
(813) 871-1819

MAIN HISPANIC NEWSPAPERS:

La Gaceta (813) 248-3921

Nuevo Siglo (813) 932-7181

OUT OF HOME:

8 sheets, 30 sheets, bulletins, mobile billboards, transit shelters, bus shelters, taxis, buses.

Icono Media (888) 584-6279

Clear Channel Outdoor
(602) 957-8116

Targeted Access Media
(212) 268-8388

Tampa Bay Jr. Posters
(813) 207-2010

20   Orlando–Daytona Beach–Melbourne, FL

Total Hispanic Population:
385,255

Average Household Income:
$39,473

Hispanic Density:
12%

NATIONALITY:

Puerto Rican	50%
Other	29%
Mexican	14%
Cuban	7%

MAIN HISPANIC TV STATIONS

Univision 26 (407) 774-2626

Telefutura 43 (407) 774-2626

Telemundo 40 (407) 888-2288

MAIN HISPANIC RADIO NETWORKS:

Florida Broadcasters
(407) 830-0800

J & V Communications
(407) 841-8282

Multicultural Radio
Broadcasting
(407) 656-9823

MAIN HISPANIC NEWSPAPERS:

Latino International Newspaper
(407) 381-9119

La Prensa (407) 767-0070

OUT OF HOME:

8 sheets, 30 sheets, bulletins, mobile billboards, transit shelters, bus shelters, taxi tops, full-wrap buses.

AdsOnPhones (301) 770-1122

Icono Media (888) 584-6279

Clear Channel Outdoor
(602) 957-8116

Targeted Access Media
(212) 268-8388

Austin, TX

 Atlanta, GA

Total Hispanic Population:
376,202

Average Household Income:
$41,638

Hispanic Density:
25.7%

NATIONALITY:
Mexican   76%
Other   24

Main Hispanic TV Stations:
Univision 31 (512) 453-8899
Telefutura 51 (512) 453-8899

MAIN HISPANIC RADIO NETWORKS:
Amigo Broadcasting
(512) 416-1100

MAIN HISPANIC NEWSPAPERS:
El Norte de Austin
(512) 448-1023

OUT OF HOME:
8 sheets, 30 sheets, bulletins,
taxi tops, bus posters.
AdsOnPhones (301) 770-1122
Icono Media (888) 584-6279
Zoom Media (212) 685-7981

Total Hispanic Population:
373,784

Average Household Income:
$50,046

Hispanic Density:
7%

NATIONALITY:
Mexican   64%
Other   30%
Puerto Rican 6%

Main Hispanic TV Stations:
Univision 34 (404) 926-2300
Telemundo 67 (N/A)

MAIN HISPANIC RADIO NETWORKS:
Ga-Mex Broadcasting
(770) 436-6171

MAIN HISPANIC NEWSPAPERS:
Mundo Hispanico
(404) 881-0441

OUT OF HOME:
8 sheets, 30 sheets, bulletins,
taxi tops, transit shelters
Icono Media (888) 584-6279

23 Boston, MA

Total Hispanic Population:
   372,007

Average Household Income:
   $41,793

Hispanic Density:
   6%

OUT OF HOME:
   8 sheets, 30 sheets, bulletins,
   taxi tops, bus posters
   AdsOnPhones (301) 770-1122
   Icono Media (888) 584-6279
   Targeted Access Media
      (212) 268-8388

NATIONALITY:

   Mexican   64%
   Other   30%
   Puerto Rican   6%

MAIN HISPANIC TV STATIONS:
   Univision 27 (781) 433-2727
   Telefutura 66 (781) 433-2727
   Telemundo 46 (N/A)

MAIN HISPANIC RADIO NETWORKS:
   Mega Communications
      (978) 458-8486
   Costa-Eagle Radio Ventures
      (978) 686-9966

MAIN HISPANIC NEWSPAPERS:
   El Mundo (617) 522-5060
   La Semana (617) 427-6212

24 Las Vegas, NV

Total Hispanic Population:
351,185

Average Household Income:
$39,887

Hispanic Density:
22.6%

OUT OF HOME:
8 sheets, 30 sheets, bulletins, lunch trucks, transit shelters

AdsOnPhones (301) 770-1122

Icono Media (888) 584-6279

Clear Channel Outdoor
(602) 957-8116

NATIONALITY:

Mexican	83%
Other	17%

MAIN HISPANIC TV STATIONS:
Univision 15 (702) 434-0015

Telefutura 27 (702) 947-2727

Telemundo 39 (702) 258-0039

MAIN HISPANIC RADIO NETWORKS:
Hispanic Broadcasting Corp.
(702) 284-6400

Entravision Communications
(702) 597-3070

MAIN HISPANIC NEWSPAPERS:
El Mundo (702) 649-8553

El Tiempo Libre
(702) 380-4504

Las Vegas Mercury
(702) 387-2993

Tucson, AZ   Corpus Christi, TX

Total Hispanic Population:
334,285

Average Household Income:
$37,298

Hispanic Density:
32.2%

NATIONALITY:

| Mexican | 83% |
| Other | 17% |

MAIN HISPANIC TV STATIONS:

Univision 3 (520) 805-1773

Telefutura 38 (520) 622-0984

Telemundo 40 (520) 322-6888

MAIN HISPANIC RADIO NETWORKS:

Lotus Communications
(520) 622-6711

Entravision Communications
(520) 325-3054

Radio Unica Communications
(520) 628-1200

Clear Channel Communications
(520) 618-2100

MAIN HISPANIC NEWSPAPERS: N/A

OUT OF HOME:

8 sheets, 30 sheets, bulletins

AdsOnPhones (301) 770-1122

Icono Media (888) 584-6279

Clear Channel Outdoor
(602) 957-8116

Total Hispanic Population:
319,799

Average Household Income:
$35,205

Hispanic Density:
57%

NATIONALITY:

| Mexican | 63% |
| Other | 37% |

MAIN HISPANIC TV STATIONS:

Univision 28 (361) 883-2823

Telefutura 41 (361) 883-2823

Telemundo 68 (361) 886-6100

MAIN HISPANIC RADIO NETWORKS:

Amigo Broadcasting
(361) 883-9830

Clear Channel Communications
(361) 289-0111

MAIN HISPANIC NEWSPAPERS: N/A

OUT OF HOME:

8 sheets, 30 sheets, bulletins

AdsOnPhones (301) 770-1122

Icono Media (888) 584-6279

Lamar Advertising
(361) 299-5550

 **Monterey–Salinas, CA**

Total Hispanic Population:
303,423

Average Household Income:
$40,194

Hispanic Density:
41.1%

NATIONALITY:

Mexican	86%
Other	14%

MAIN HISPANIC TV STATIONS:

Univision 67 (408) 373-6767

Caballero 3 (972) 503-6800

MAIN HISPANIC RADIO NETWORKS:

Hispanic Broadcasting Corp.
(559) 456-4000

Entravision Communications
(830) 771-9950

Moon Broadcasting
(916) 646-4000

MAIN HISPANIC NEWSPAPERS:

El Sol (831) 757-8118

OUT OF HOME:

30 sheets, bulletins, king-size bus posters in Salinas only

AdsOnPhones (301) 770-1122

Icono Media (888) 584-6279

Clear Channel Outdoor
(602) 957-8116

28 **Bakersfield, CA**

Total Hispanic Population:
258,869

Average Household Income:
$42,365

Hispanic Density:
43.6%

NATIONALITY:

Mexican	83%
Other	17%

MAIN HISPANIC TV STATIONS:

Univision 39 & 45
(661) 324-0031

Telefutura 52 (661) 324-0031

MAIN HISPANIC RADIO NETWORKS:

Lotus Communications
(661) 721-1010

MAIN HISPANIC NEWSPAPERS:

El Mexicalo (805) 323-9334

OUT OF HOME:

8 sheets, 30 sheets, bulletins.

AdsOnPhones (301) 770-1122

Icono Media (888) 584-6279

 **29** Seattle–
Tacoma, WA

 30 Portland, OR

Total Hispanic Population:
257,890

Average Household Income:
$40,846

Hispanic Density:
5.9%

NATIONALITY:

Mexican   68%

Other   26%

Puerto Rican   6%

MAIN HISPANIC TV STATIONS: N/A

MAIN HISPANIC RADIO NETWORKS:

FTP Corporation
(253) 476-5944

Multicultural Radio
Broadcasting
(206) 292-7800

MAIN HISPANIC NEWSPAPERS:

El Mundo (509) 663-5737

OUT OF HOME:

30 sheets, bulletins, king-size
bus posters

Icono Media (888) 584-6279

Total Hispanic Population:
251,996

Average Household Income:
$43,094

Hispanic Density:
8.9%

NATIONALITY:

Mexican   78%

Other   22%

MAIN HISPANIC TV STATIONS: N/A

MAIN HISPANIC RADIO NETWORKS:

Pacific NW Broadcasting
(503) 227-2156

Sanlee Broadcasting
Corporation
(503) 769-1460

MAIN HISPANIC NEWSPAPERS:

El Hispanic News
(503) 228-3139

Noticias Latinas
(503) 227-7780

OUT OF HOME:

30 sheets, bulletins, king-size
bus posters, full tail buses,
transit shelters

Icono Media (888) 584-627

Looking Forward

Woods & Poole projects that the top three Hispanic markets in the country will remain the same through 2015, but there will be some minor shifts among those ranking fourth and below. Note that Bakersfield which was number 30 in 2000 ranks 31st in 2005. Also, note that by 2015, the top 30 markets will have as many Hispanics as there were in 2000 in the United States, including Puerto Rico.

Top-30 Hispanic Markets in 2005

Hispanic population in millions

Rank 2000	Rank 2005	Name	2000	2005	2010	2015
1	1	Los Angeles	6.6	7.6	8.5	9.3
2	2	New York	3.8	4.3	4.7	5.1
3	3	Miami–Ft. Lauderdale	1.6	1.9	2.2	2.4
4	5	Houston	1.4	1.8	2.1	2.4
5	4	Chicago	1.5	1.8	1.9	2.1
6	7	Dallas–Ft. Worth	1.2	1.5	1.8	2.0
7	6	San Francisco–Oakland–San Jose	1.3	1.5	1.6	1.8
8	9	Phoenix	0.9	1.2	1.5	1.7
9	8	San Antonio	1.0	1.2	1.3	1.5
10	10	Harlingen–Weslaco–Brownsville–McAllen	0.9	1.0	1.1	1.2
11	11	San Diego	0.8	0.9	1.1	1.2
12	13	Sacramento–Stockton–Modesto	0.7	0.9	1.1	1.3
13	12	Fresno–Visalia	0.8	0.9	1.0	1.1
14	16	Denver	0.6	0.7	0.9	1.0
15	14	El Paso	0.7	0.7	0.8	0.9
16	15	Albuquerquec–Santa Fe	0.6	0.7	0.8	0.9
17	18	Washington, DC (Hagerstown)	0.5	0.6	0.7	0.8
18	17	Philadelphia	0.5	0.6	0.7	0.8
19	19	Tampa–St. Petersburg (Sarasota)	0.4	0.5	0.6	0.8
20	22	Orlando–Daytona Beach–Melbourne	0.4	0.5	0.6	0.8
21	23	Atlanta	0.3	0.5	0.6	0.6
22	21	Austin	0.4	0.5	0.6	0.7
23	20	Boston (Manchester)	0.4	0.4	0.5	0.6
24	26	Las Vegas	0.3	0.4	0.5	0.6
25	24	Tucson (Sierra Vista)	0.3	0.4	0.5	0.5
26	25	Corpus Christi	0.3	0.3	0.4	0.4
27	27	Monterey–Salinas	0.3	0.3	0.4	0.4
28	29	Portland, OR	0.2	0.3	0.4	0.5
29	28	Seattle-Tacoma	0.2	0.3	0.4	0.5
30	31	Salt Lake City	0.2	0.3	0.4	0.4
		30-Market Total	**29.1**	**34.5**	**39.7**	**44.3**

Source: *The Complete Economic and Demographic Data Source (CEDDS)*, 2004. © Woods & Poole Economics, Inc., Washington, DC; www.woodsandpoole.com (see page 134)

13

Hispanic Youth

We have now begun the hunt for the white tiger, for the holy grail, for the black orchid of the U.S. Hispanic market: the often seen, but seldom captured, Hispanic youth. No other aspect of capturing the U.S. Hispanic market has engendered as much interest or evoked as much terror as the idea of actively going after the youth audience.

This interest and terror is as true of major multinational corporations as it is of small- and medium-sized companies. Many have ventured into these murky waters without success and returned no wiser. So why keep doing it? Why continue to try to capture this elusive target?

Well, for starters, I'll remind you that the Hispanic consumer segment is younger than the mainstream segment and growing at a much faster clip than the mainstream segment, that Hispanics tend to be more brand loyal, and that they regard word of mouth very highly. All of this means that by capturing Hispanic teens and tweens you are establishing a significant foothold in the marketplace and ensuring the health of your business.

To accomplish this all you have to do is figure out how to communicate with a population that is as complex and fickle as any young group of people, with the added complications of cultural ambiguity, language-fluency issues, and an almost preternatural ability to smell stereotypical, trite, and condescending marketing. What few people realize is that, unlike mainstream youth, Hispanic youth are exposed to advertising and marketing in two languages. They see and hear the difference in quality of production and in creative thinking between mainstream-English advertising and Spanish-language advertising.

So let's get started. To begin with, the most important thing you need to understand about the U.S. Hispanic youth market is that they are not a sub-segment of the at-large U.S. Hispanic market. They are 65 to 70 percent bilingual or English preferred, consume a significant amount of English-language media, and are mostly born in the United States. These things mean that they think differently and function differently than the at-large Hispanic market.

For our purposes, it means we have to treat them and think about them differently if we are to sell to them. If you are going to be successful selling to U.S. Hispanic youth consumers, you need to make sure that you do not sell to them as U.S. Hispanic youth consumers. Confused?

Let's explore it. As you have read previously, when you are developing a campaign or effort to sell to Hispanics in the U.S. you need to demonstrate a modicum of understanding of the culture in order to make your consumers feel welcome and feel you care about them, their culture, and where they come from. With Hispanic youth the way to demonstrate this is by trying not to demonstrate these things in your communications in obvious or contrived ways. What would engender nostalgia or a sense of pride in a foreign-born, older consumer might breed a negative reaction from a Hispanic teen, who would see through the attempt at demonstrating cultural insight and that you "really get it." Let's take a closer look at Hispanic teens.

The Wonderful and Lucrative Enigma of the Hispanic Teen

In recent years, a number of companies have tried to understand, segment and target the Hispanic teen market. With market competition in traditional teen categories such as sportswear (jeans), sports drinks, carbonated soft drinks, health and beauty, and snacks reaching a fever pitch, marketers want to find alternative market segments for growth. It is no secret that the Hispanic market as a whole is a fertile ground for any marketer who takes the time to properly target it.

Hispanic teens, however, present an even more significant opportunity. Demographically, Hispanic teens are a force to be reckoned with and will be even more so in the coming decades. Hispanics under age 20 account for more than 38 percent of the total Hispanic population in the united States. That is more than 12 million Hispanic youths. Any marketer who has delved into the teen market can attest that it is difficult to gauge teenagers in general. Trying to discern fads from trends from cycles can make anybody's head spin. This is one area that Nostradamus did well to stay away from. The lure of the Y or echo generation is the same as that of the baby boomers back in the 1970s.

Capture them now, create a bond with your brand, remain relevant to the market as they pass through different life stages and watch your brand grow right along with them. Throw in some social ambiguity, political awakening, language-of-preference issues, and burgeoning cultural pride, and you have the Hispanic teen market.

Given myriad issues to understand and overcome, almost every marketer who has an interest in marketing to Hispanic teens has been asking, "Why should I do anything different for Hispanic teens? They mostly speak English and watch TV in English. Why can't I just assume that they are being reached through my general market campaign?"

This is a valid question and one that, until recently, had no real answer. Researchers who have analyzed this market in depth have been unable to provide a true answer to those companies that are looking to develop relevant campaigns. A dressed-up regurgitation of census data or reporting of well-known demographic tidbits has been insufficient to give true strategic guidance to navigate such a precarious but potentially lucrative market.

The key may lie in throwing out the psychographic and social paradigm into which marketers, ad agencies, and researchers alike have been trying to fit Hispanic teens. A number of recent marketing efforts targeting this segment have provided some fresh insight into just exactly who Hispanic teens are.

For starters, Hispanic teens should be considered a free-standing, separate, and distinct market from the at-large U.S. Hispanic market. Hispanic teens in the U.S. are attitudinally different, most speak their own brand of Spanish ("Spanglish"), and are U.S.-born, yet they are usually lumped together with an at-large U.S. Hispanic market that is traditionally defined as being Spanish-dominant, foreign-born, and well defined from a cultural standpoint.

Does this mean that decades of findings from the U.S. Hispanic market should be ignored when it comes to Hispanic teens? Of course not; there are obvious crossovers and cultural insights that are not only relevant, but crucial to understanding this segment. What it does mean is that capturing the Hispanic teen market will require a fresh and innovative approach that relies on a new strategic tack and not on a forced cultural model.

A Demographic Awakening

Most U.S.-Hispanic teens begin the process of defining themselves culturally by the age of 16. At this age a burgeoning cultural pride begins to take hold, and these teens begin the process of retro-acculturation. Recently, however, researchers have begun to notice that retro-acculturation is beginning at an earlier age than in the past.

Across a number of categories, kids as young as age 11 express the strong desire to learn more about their culture and the traditions that go along with it. Although it is much too early to tell, some researchers believe that this is due to two main factors:

- Hispanic teens are undergoing a demographic awakening. They are becoming more aware of their numbers within their communities and across the United States. They are better educated and more informed than their parents and realize their enormous purchasing power

- There is no other way to put it: being part of an ethnic group is "in." In examining trends over the past five years, researchers have discovered that within most of the urban centers across the U.S. it is the ethnic teens who set the trends.

How to Reach Them

With such an enigmatic and potentially lucrative market segment, the $64,000 question is "How do you reach them?"

For years now, Hispanic advertising agency creatives have been spinning their wheels to come up with marketing communications that reach this segment. This is especially difficult because in this case you have a teen segment basically divided into two very different groups. On the one hand, you have younger Hispanic teens (aged 13 to 16), who are culturally ambiguous and difficult to get to commit to anything. It is hard for them to decide if they want to be Hispanic or not, let alone what form of communication or execution they find most relevant or appealing. On the other hand, you have the older teens (aged 16–19), who are beginning to define themselves culturally and for whom being authentic and legit is crucial to their social standing.

So how do you develop culturally relevant marketing communications and materials for both of these groups? The answer may be as simple as: You can't, and you shouldn't try to. From a return-on-investment standpoint, marketers are always looking for the most bang for their buck. Therefore, from a purely ROI standpoint, splitting the Hispanic teen market into two groups in order to develop relevant communications for each is obviously not the best answer. The answer may lie in making certain concessions and redefining the Hispanic teen market. In looking at the demographic and psychographic makeup of the younger Hispanic teen segment, marketers and ad agencies may have to concede the point and acknowledge that, from a fiscal standpoint, younger Hispanic teens (13–16) can more effectively be reached through mainstream, English-language media.

However, this is only half of the answer. The other half may lie in redefining the Hispanic youth market to include young adults (aged 20–22). This makes sense not only from a fiscal standpoint, but also from a cultural one. Hispanic young adults are perhaps the most culturally aware and sensitive of all Hispanic segments. They are what the Hispanic teens strive to be. They are also the age group where the teens looking for role models. Older sisters, brothers, cousins and uncles are invariably brought up when teens are asked about people they admire and wish to emulate.

Looking at the median age of the Hispanic market (age 28), at the projected purchasing power of Hispanics as a whole ($371 billion) and at their demographic presence (15 percent of total U.S. population), it is not difficult to realize the promise this market holds. One thing is certain: Only those companies willing to take a fresh approach and willing to challenge some of the established boundaries will truly benefit from the wonderful and lucrative enigma that is the Hispanic teen.

14

The Other Half and Hidden Treasure

I
n the beginning, we established that we would be focusing on the Spanish-dominant, less-acculturated U.S. Hispanic audience, but what about the other half? What about those people who speak English, but still define themselves as Hispanic? Let's take a look, shall we?

As Hispanic influence on mainstream America continues to grow and more bilingual and English-dominant Hispanic consumers return to their cultural roots, Hispanic marketing may be the best value out there. We have seen that the U.S. Hispanic market holds a substantial potential for significant market-share increases and improved bottom lines for those companies willing to make the financial and organizational commitment required. As we have noted, a significant number of U.S. marketers are already either in the midst of developing and implementing their Hispanic marketing plans or considering their first foray into the market.

As they do this, however, most may be missing one of the most profound developments in the remarkable evolution of the U.S. Hispanic market. In addition to a marked increase in the level of sophistication of the U.S. Hispanic consumer across a host of categories, there has been a redefinition of exactly what the U.S. "Hispanic market" encompasses. Historically, marketers and Hispanic experts alike have defined the Hispanic market as being principally composed of foreign-born, Spanish-dominant or -dependent consumers. As defined earlier in this book, Spanish–dominant describes an individual who, although understanding and speaking some English, functions predominantly in Spanish. Spanish–dependent describes an individual whose English-language skills are so limited that he or she can only function in Spanish.

Although the U.S. Hispanic population is composed of individuals from a much broader range of ethnic and language-preference backgrounds, including bilingual and English-dominant/preferred individuals, the definition of the U.S. Hispanic segment in a marketing context has historically been determined by the language in which Hispanics watch and listen to media and by cultural relevance issues. Marketers and ad agencies alike have functioned under the assumption that it is the Spanish-dominant and Spanish-dependent consumers who should define a U.S. Hispanic marketing effort. After all, they reason, any U.S. Hispanic consumers who fall into the bilingual, English-dominant and English-dependent categories are being reached through English-language, general-market communication efforts and media vehicles (the general market being the at-large, "nonethnic" marketplace).

While this line of thought is based on sound reasoning and appears to make perfect sense, it does not reflect the true dynamics of today's U.S. Hispanic marketplace and may lead marketers to leave a sizable portion of the U.S. Hispanic opportunity on the table. Remember that bilingual or English-speaking Hispanics represent almost half of the U.S. Hispanic population. This means that by defining the U.S. Hispanic market as being composed only of Spanish-dominant or -preferred consumers, marketers are discounting almost half of the U.S. Hispanic population by assuming they are already being reached through general-market efforts.

A Cultural Shift

While marketing efforts targeting the Spanish-speaking component of the marketplace have been increasing not only in quantity, but also in quality, the English-speaking component of the same marketplace has, until now, been all but ignored by corporate America. There is a reason for that, however. Most U.S.-born Hispanics over age 20 struggled with the issue of ethnicity at one time or another in their lifetimes. This struggle usually took place during the crucial teen years. While all young people, regardless of ethnic background, have to deal with defining themselves both socially and emotionally, U.S. Hispanic teens have also had to struggle with the issue of defining themselves culturally. For many, that struggle has led to a suppression or dilution of their Hispanic cultural roots. This suppression manifests itself throughout their maturation process and contributes to the way they define themselves later on in life.

For instance, in the past many teens would change their name to its Anglo version and would refuse to speak in Spanish outside the home. As they grew and matured into adults, and in order to maintain legitimacy through consistency, some of these young people continued to refuse to speak Spanish, adopt more Anglo customs, and function, in essence, as general-market consumers. Political and social issues that have been perceived as being anti-immigrant or anti-Hispanic have only served to exacerbate and ultimately perpetuate this dynamic. This all plays back to the whole acculturation and retro-acculturation model we discussed in Chapter 6.

In the past five years, however, a number of factors have spurred a marked shift in the cultural definition process that U.S. Hispanics go through. While manifesting itself most clearly in the teenage population, this shift has also begun to effect a change in the way U.S. Hispanic adults define themselves. All of a sudden Ralph Smith-Gomes is once again Rafael Gomez, and Sofia Alvarez, who claimed to be from Iowa and to speak only a little Spanish, is telling anyone who will listen about her great-great-grandfather's role in the Mexican revolution and she speaks Spanish fluently. While still in its early stages, this shift signals a profound change in how U.S. marketers will need to define and address the U.S. Hispanic market.

Why All of a Sudden?

While the effects of it are only now being felt, the factors that have combined to create this condition have been in motion for over 20 years. A continuous influx of immigrants, a larger household size, an extremely young population, and higher birth rates have all been present over the past two decades and are only now beginning to tip the scale. Although the increase in influence begins with the numbers that all of these factors add up to (remember that U.S. Hispanics number nearly 38 million at last count, are growing faster than other populations and are the second-largest U.S. population), it goes on to encompass much more. From the most recent foreign-born arrival to the U.S.-born, third-generation segment, life for a U.S. Hispanic is most definitely an easier proposition now than it was only five years ago. That is because in addition to a demographic explosion, the culture itself is being not only accepted, but also embraced.

Unless you have had your head stuck under a rock over the past two years, you have probably noticed the increased influence that the Latino culture is having on at-large U.S. popular culture. From entertainment to politics to sports, the Hispanic influence is clear, significant and growing every day.

I pointed out earlier that baseball, America's favorite pastime, is now replete with Hispanic surnames, some of which belong to some of the most dominant players. Alex Rodriguez, an infielder formerly with the Seattle Mariners, signed a contract worth over $250 million with the Texas Rangers, the most lucrative contract in sports history. The U.S. Hispanic vote was hotly contested in the presidential election and the state that ultimately decided the election, Florida, has a huge Cuban and South/Central American population. Ricky Martin, Cristina Aguilera, Marc Anthony and Shakira are but a few of the artists that have taken the music industry by storm. Jessica Alba starred in one of the 2000 season's hottest new shows, *Dark Angel,* and Penelope Cruz is becoming a hot commodity on the silver screen.

These are only the most obvious examples of the growing Latino influence, but more subtle examples abound across America and are beginning to redefine the traditional notion of the U.S. Hispanic market. All of this has served to engender a very Hispanic-friendly environment in the U.S., regardless of place of birth, ethnic makeup or language preference. The bottom line is that being Hispanic is "in," and everyone who can make the claim wants to be a part of it. That means not only Spanish-preferred U.S. Hispanics, but all U.S. Hispanics.

Besides effecting a change in the cultural definition process that young people go through, the Hispanic influence has engendered an ever-growing sense of pride and is prompting bilingual and English–dominant, U.S. Hispanic adults to return to their roots and embrace their cultural heritage. As they continue to redefine themselves and to return to their cultural roots, the often ignored and under-served English-speaking segment of the U.S. Hispanic population will be looking to see themselves reflected and considered in the communications marketers have developed to reach them.

But They Understand My Message!

The most persuasive arguments in marketing tend to be budget-driven, and this one is no different. The argument might be "Why spend money and time addressing a group of people that I have been addressing all along? Since they speak and understand English, they can hear and understand my message now without me having to spend one additional penny."

While this argument is logical and has until now been persuasive, it does not reflect the true essence of what marketing communication is ultimately all about, effecting a change and selling a product. That change may be increased purchase intent, increased awareness, or—even better—a connection between consumer and brand, the "That brand is for me!" moment that creatives, account executives, and strategists alike all work for. It is the moment that positively affects how the consumer feels or behaves in the context of the brands the marketing team represents. All would most likely agree that for this to happen, the consumer must not only understand the message, but must identify with it in some way. It is only after the identification takes place that the advertising begins to pay off, either in awareness or in dollars and cents.

The best parallel to draw is that of the African-American market. When looking to target the African–American market, U.S. marketers look to the cultural component of the market, not the language of preference, in order to develop relevant communications. An argument could be made that, since African-Americans understand English, general-market communications should be enough to address them. Although that may have been the mentality that prevailed prior to the late 1980s, the 1990s hip-hop culture brought about significant change and helped to establish culturally relevant marketing as the only way to communicate legitimacy to African-American and urban youth. African-Americans were finally recognized as a viable and distinct market that required culturally relevant communications be developed for them.

The success of brands like Sprite, Gap and FUBU, as well as the resurgence of brands like Adidas speaks volumes about the value of developing advertising specifically targeting African-American and urban youth. These brands discovered that by developing culturally authentic, urban advertising they were doing more than appealing to the African-American and urban segments. Much more. As the hip-hop generation's influence grew, so did the brands that were relevant to that generation. Across the country, from suburban white America to Hispanic America, consumers adopted the culture, the music, the style, and the image that came with hip-hop. It defined an entire generation of young consumers. What resulted was a bonanza for those marketers who had the vision to recognize the opportunity and to do something about it.

Amazingly, an opportunity that shows up once in a lifetime if a marketer is lucky is showing up again. The English-speaking, U.S. Hispanic market is no different than the African-American market of the early 1990s. It is a culturally distinct segment that represents close to half of the entire U.S. Hispanic population and that has been almost completely ignored by marketers' U.S. Hispanic efforts, which have until now been almost exclusively Spanish-language driven.

There is an opportunity for U.S. marketers and small businesses to communicate with these consumers in a more relevant, legitimate way, to develop communications that acknowledge them as a part of a distinct group of people and a culture whose influence on the American fabric is only going to continue to grow. It is very likely that by doing this, marketers will not only be addressing a segment of the U.S. Hispanic market that until now has gone completely ignored, but will also be developing marketing communications that are perceived as different, fun, and appealing by their general market consumers as well.

Moreover, since the English–speaking segment is a segment that has always existed and been accounted for as part of the general market, from a budgetary standpoint, it does not require additional funds, but a reallocation of them. As with the hip-hop culture of the 1990s, the real opportunity lies in understanding where the influence on American popular culture is coming from and capitalizing on it. It is patently clear that a significant part of that influence is now and will in the future be coming from the U.S. Hispanic population.

To capitalize on the opportunity marketers will need to recognize that language is just one component of the cultural definition of the U.S. Hispanic market. Perhaps the most obvious and immediate question, and justifiably so, might be "Why didn't my Hispanic agency tell me about all this?" The answer is that for most Hispanic agencies budgetary realities dictate where and how they concentrate their efforts. Although improving in the past two years, the U.S. Hispanic marketing budgets for most major U.S. marketers are often a small fraction of the company's overall marketing budget. U.S. Hispanic agencies are thus forced to concentrate their efforts on a market that has not been addressed at all by U.S. marketers, the Spanish-dominant/preferred market.

Unfortunately, this budgetary reality has over the years defined the U.S. Hispanic opportunity for most marketers. Budgetary constraints, however, are most likely not the only culprit. Some U.S. Hispanic agencies, fearing a loss of business to their bigger and better-funded general-market counterparts, have probably also restricted their definition of the marketplace to the Spanish-dominant, U.S. Hispanic consumers. The thinking may have been that if the definition of the U.S. Hispanic market is broadened to encompass the English-speaking segment, general-market agencies will not only be able to command a share of the Hispanic budget, but will also be able to make inroads into what has been traditionally the Hispanic ad agency's space. Additionally, Hispanic agencies may fear that general-market agencies, seeing the enormous potential of the market, will look to better establish their Hispanic credentials in order to completely take over that part of the business as well. The reality, however, is quite different.

During the 1990's hip–hop boom, most marketers recognized the need for partners that understood the cultural nuances of the hip-hop culture and that could develop truly authentic and legitimate communications targeting that culture. It should be no different for the English-speaking, Hispanic market. In fact, that is precisely the essence of the opportunity: addressing English-language Hispanic consumers through culturally charged marketing communications. Most marketers will probably realize that the best place to get that type of cultural insight is from their Hispanic ad agency and not from their general-market agency. Most marketers also will likely recognize the fact that although their general-market agency can develop marketing communications that English-speaking Hispanics can understand (they have been doing that all along), they cannot provide the subtle nuances that make these communications truly relevant. And finally, most marketers are likely to recognize that they do not need to come up with additional money, and they do not need to take money from their current Hispanic efforts in order to address this new market.

Since this is a segment historically included in the "general market" budget, marketers need only reallocate some of that budget to this newly defined segment. What is patently clear is that from a return-on-investment standpoint, Hispanic marketing is very hard to beat. It is also clear that the growing influence of the Hispanic culture on U.S. popular culture will provide plenty of opportunities for those marketers with the vision to recognize that what will be needed to appeal to the Hispanic market of the 21st century will be more about something the Hispanic market truly cares about than about something that it can simply understand.

15

So Here We Are

We have come to the end of our little journey. It wasn't that hard, was it? I hope that the information contained in this book has inspired you to pursue a relationship with the U.S. Hispanic audience.

Besides the obvious monetary value to your business, I believe that the U.S. Hispanic audience can represent a solid base of support for your brand, product, or service. I also think that in the process of learning about the culture and trying to communicate with its members you will also gain a perspective about a unique and vibrant culture that is every day becoming a more important component of our popular culture here in the United States.

The U.S. Hispanic population is not just a consumer population. It is moms and dads sending their kids to war; it is students breaking a cycle of poverty and despair; it is professionals contributing some of the best thinking of our era; and it is a culture of warm and friendly neighbors, friends, brothers and sisters that will undoubtedly play a critical role in shaping America's future.

I for one have never been more proud to be Hispanic and felt more American. *Buena suerte y hasta luego*!

A Voice from the Trenches

I wanted to make sure that within this book I also included the experience of someone working at a major corporation. I felt that the individual should be someone that was not Hispanic because I wanted to convey the point that you don't have to be Hispanic to be successful selling to Hispanics. Greg Knipp is exactly the voice I was looking for. He has had the opportunity of working to sell to Hispanics on the agency side and also working for a Fortune 500 company.

I think you will find some of the lessons he learned along the way to be interesting and informative. I believe that the most compelling aspect of his story is that he was able to recognize the business value of the market; he was able to identify the aspects of the Hispanic culture that would make their efforts succeed from the perspective of the customer and he was able to figure out what went wrong when situation changed. In the end it is about figuring out how you can present whatever it is that you sell—product or service—into what the Hispanic consumer is looking for. Enjoy!

Case Study: Frito-Lay

When Juan first asked me to write a chapter for his book, I wasn't sure of the value I could bring. Juan is the expert on Hispanic marketing. I am a white guy from Kansas. Growing up, my only exposure to the Hispanic culture was watching *Chico and the Man* and taking Spanish classes in high school. But, then I realized that if someone with my background can have some success marketing to U.S. Hispanics, anyone can.

A little more about my background, I have spent the majority of my career working in advertising, first for the Leo Burnett Company and now for a Hispanic marketing agency in Dallas. I also spent about four years working for Frito-Lay. I was a part of the first Hispanic marketing team at Frito-Lay and was responsible for execution of the national launch of Frito-Lay's initial foray into Hispanic marketing. What I quickly learned, with the help of some very good advice from our Hispanic marketing agency, was that marketing to Hispanics was all about common sense, despite how some try to complicate the process.

What follows is an overly complex approach to Hispanic marketing planning that recently came across my desk.

- Identify the needs of the Hispanic market as they relate to the categories in which you compete.

- Assess the volume opportunity.

- Assess your company's license to succeed within the market.
  a. Does or can your product portfolio satisfy the needs of the market?
  b. Is your brand promise relevant?
  c. Are there opportunities to line extend or flank your current brand offerings to better appeal to the Hispanic market?
  d. Do we have distribution in the appropriate channels and with key customers that target the Hispanic market?
  e. Do you have research, advertising and promotion agency partners that are experienced and capable to assess and communicate to a Hispanic audience?

- Define success and how you will measure it.

While perfectly correct, the marketing speak could scare off the most experienced of marketers. In my opinion, it is much more simple. It all of this boils down to:

- Do Hispanics use a product or service like that which you sell?

- Does your product or service satisfy their needs?

- If not, can the product or service be altered in some way to better satisfy their needs?

- What return would you expect to receive on your efforts to market to Hispanics?

This is the process we followed at Frito-Lay and for a while we had some great success, but we still managed to over-complicate things as we progressed. I've realized that my experience may be a good case study in both how and how not to approach Hispanic marketing. We did quite a bit right in year one of our efforts and quite a bit wrong in year two.

What Went Right and What Went Wrong

First let me tell you about what I believe we did right. The team at Frito-Lay determined the Hispanic market was a huge opportunity. The market was growing. Buying power was increasing exponentially. Hispanic families were larger and younger. And, most importantly, these families ate more salty snacks. Unfortunately, they weren't all Frito-Lay products. We determined that while salty snacks appealed to the U.S. Hispanic market, our products, specifically the flavors offered, failed to fully satisfy what the market was looking for.

We looked to our Mexican subsidiary, Sabritas, for ideas on new flavors and products that could better deliver. We launched Doritos Salsa Verde, Fritos Sabrositas, Lay's Adobadas and new Flamin' Hot Cheetos to target the needs of the Hispanic market. These were all among the most successful brands and flavors at Sabritas.

Efforts supporting the programs included consumer advertising and both consumer and trade promotion, including a World Cup soccer promotion. We spent millions behind the national launch and made somewhere in the neighborhood of eight dollars of profit for every dollar invested. It was the best option and we capitalized upon the opportunity.

Then, somewhere between year one execution and year two planning, we lost it. We became so excited by what was a great business building opportunity that we lost track of what made us successful—providing a product that was preferred by Hispanics. We went from a structured, strategic approach to hurried, unfocused, throw it at the wall and see what sticks. Some of what we threw at the wall stuck, like Lay's Limon. This product was another example of stealing a good idea that was proven successful by Sabritas in Mexico. Where we got off track was where we chose to place our big bets, things like Doritos Smoky Red Barbeque. Get this: take an unappealing flavor, make it impossible to translate and then adapt advertising with absolutely no relevance to the market. This is not a good idea and it failed miserably.

After a couple of years of recovery, Frito-Lay is back to a very successful marketing model, providing a product that satisfies the snack cravings of Hispanics better than anyone else. It has expanded its Hispanic product portfolio and is enjoying a great deal of success.

The learning is, again, pretty simple:

- Make sure you are offering a product or service that Hispanics want or need.

- Make changes to your product or service if you need to in order to better appeal to Hispanics.

- By all means, do not try to force feed your product or service to this market simply because the population is growing.

- Keep it simple.

Chambers of Commerce, Resources, and Contacts

This is a directory of selected Hispanic Business and Chamber of Commerce (C of C) organizations. Information given here was correct as this book went to its second printing in February 2005.

Alabama

Alabama Hispanic C of C
  1901 6th Avenue North, Suite 3120
  Birmingham AL 35203
  Phone (866) 763-3667
  Fax (205) 322-2045

Arizona

Arizona Hispanic C of C
  255 East Osborn Rd., Suite 201
  Phoenix, AZ 85012
  Phone (602) 279-1800
  Fax (602) 279-8900

Border Trade Alliance
  111 West Monroe, Suite 510
  Phoenix, AZ 85003
  Phone (602) 266-7427
  Fax (602) 266-9826

Nogales Santa Cruz County C of C
  123 West Kino Park Way
  Nogales, AZ 85621
  Phone (520) 287-3685
  Fax (520) 287-3688

Tucson Hispanic C of C
  823 East Speedway Blvd.
  Tucson, AZ 85719
  Phone (520) 620-0005
  Fax (520) 620-9685

California

Antelope Valley Hispanic C of C
  38434 9th Street East, Suite J
  Palmdale, CA 93550
  Phone 661-538-0607
  Fax (661) 538-1057

California Hispanic C of C
  770 L Street Suite 1230
  Sacramento, CA 95814
  Phone (916) 444-2221
  Fax (916) 669-2870

Camara De Comercio De Marin
  P.O. Box 3359
  San Rafael, CA 94912
  Phone (415) 456-9379
  Fax (415) 507-2101

Central California Hispanic C of C
  2331 Fresno Street
  Fresno, CA 93721
  Phone (559) 485-6640
  Fax (559) 495-4811

Coachella Valley Mexican-American C of C
  P.O. Box 1874
  Indio, CA 92202
  Phone (760) 347-9402
  Fax (760) 347-4288

Fresno Hispanic C of C
  1456 West Shaw Avenue
  Fresno, CA, 93711
  Phone (559) 222-8705
  Fax (888) 222-8706

Fontana Hispanic C of C
  P.O. Box 3944
  Fontana, CA 92334
  Phone (909) 428-6797
  Fax (909) 428-6797

Gilroy Hispanic C of C
  P.O. Box 1312
  Gilroy, CA 95021
  Phone (408) 225-5053
  Fax (408) 846-6598

Greater Corona Hispanic C of C
  119 East 4th Street
  Corona, CA 92879
  Phone (909) 371-0955
  Fax (909) 737-5668

Greater Riverside Hispanic C of C
  P.O. Box 5872
  Riverside, CA 92517
  Phone (909) 682-7422
  Fax (775) 890-8520

Greater San Jose Hispanic C of C
Entrepreneur Center
  84 West Santa Clara Street, Suite 100
  San Jose, CA 95113
  Phone (408) 494-0296
  Fax (408) 494-0291

Greater Stockton Hispanic C of C
  445 West Weber Avenue, Suite 220
  Stockton, CA 95203
  Phone (209) 943-6117
  Fax (209) 466-5271

Hispanic C of C Alameda County
  1840 Embarcadero, Suite 101
  Oakland, CA 94606
  Phone (510) 536-4477
  Fax (510) 536-4320

Hispanic Chamber Alliance of California
  900 Wilshire Blvd., Suite 624
  Los Angeles, CA 90017
  Phone (213) 239-0984
  Fax (213) 612-3616

Hispanic C of C of the City and
County of Merced
  1640 North Street, Suite 220
  Merced, CA 95340
  Phone (209) 384-9537
  Fax (209) 723-5051

Hispanic C of C of Contra Costa County
  2255 Morello Ave #150
  Pleasant Hill, CA 94523
  Phone (925) 281-2623
  Fax (925) 281-2623

Hispanic C of C of Orange County
  2323 North Broadway, Suite 305
  Santa Ana, CA 92706
  Phone (714) 953-4289
  Fax (714) 953-0273

Hispanic C of C of Marin
  P.O. Box 4423
  San Rafael, CA 94913
  Phone (415) 721-9686
  Fax (415) 479-4587

Hispanic Chamber of Monterey County
  5 East Gabilan Street, Suite 214
  Salinas, CA 93901
  Phone (831) 757-1251
  Fax (831) 757-1246

Hispanic C of C Solano/Napa County
  P.O. Box 2723
  Fairfield, CA 94533
  Phone (707) 643-5037

Hispanic C of C Silicon Valley
  696 East Santa Clara Street, Suite 106
  San Jose, CA 95112
  Phone (408) 213-0320
  Fax (408) 213-0329

Hispanic Chamber of Ventura County
  937 West Fifth Street
  Oxnard, CA 93032
  Phone (805) 486-0266

Hispanic C of C of Yolo County
  P.O. Box 1232
  Woodland, CA 95776
  Phone (530) 666-5335
  Fax (530) 406-8880

Inland Empire Hispanic C of C
  320 North E Street, Suite 211
  San Bernandino, CA 92401
  Phone (909) 888-2188
  Fax (909) 888-1151

International C of C of San Ysidro
  522 East San Ysidro Blvd.
  San Ysidro, CA 92173
  Phone (619) 428-9530
  Fax (619) 428-9467

Kern County Hispanic C of C
  1401 19th Street, Suite 110
  Bakersfield, CA 93301
  Phone (661) 633-5495
  Fax (661) 633-5499

Latin Business Association
  5120 South San Pedro Street
  Suite 530 Little Tokyo
  Los Angeles, CA 90012
  Phone (323) 721-4000
  Fax (323) 722-5050

Latino C of C of Compton
  P.O. Box 449
  Compton, CA 90223
  Phone (310) 639-4455
  Fax (310) 639-4455

Madera Hispanic C of C
  11110 El Capital Dr.
  Madera, CA 93638
  Phone (559) 674-8821
  Fax (559) 674-9084

Mexico-USA Economic Partnership Council
  2557 Flintridge Dr.
  Glendale, CA 91206
  Phone (323) 255-2083
  Fax (323) 255-0040

Perris Valley C of C
  11 South D Street
  Perris, CA 92570
  Phone (909) 657-3555

Pomona Valley Latino C of C
  142 East Third Street
  Pomona, CA 91766
  Phone (909) 469-0702
  Fax (909) 469-0604

Regional Hispanic C of C
  One World Trade Center, Suite 420
  Long Beach, CA 90831
  Phone and *Fax* (562) 597-7298

Sacramento Hispanic C of C
  2848 Arden Way, Suite 230
  Sacramento, CA 95825
  Phone (916) 486-7708
  Fax (916) 486-7728

Santa Barbara Hispanic C of C
P.O. Box 6592
Santa Barbara, CA, 93160
Phone (888) 560-1686
Fax (888) 560-1686

San Benito County Hispanic C of C
449 San Benito Street, Suite 28
Hollister, CA 95023
Phone (831) 638-1163
Fax (831) 638-1026

San Diego County Hispanic C of C
1250 Sixth Avenue, Suite 550
San Diego, CA 92101
Phone (619) 702-0790
Fax (619) 696-3282

San Mateo County Hispanic C of C
812 Palm Avenue
Redwood City, CA 94061
Phone (650) 839-1369
Fax (650)-839-2009

South Bay Latino C of C
P.O. Box 452391
Los Angeles, CA 90045
Phone (310) 676-2568
Fax (310) 676-2568

South San Joaquin Hispanic C of C
P.O. Box 475
Manteca, CA 95336
Phone (209) 239-4424
Fax (209) 825-7162

Stanislaus County Hispanic C of C
1114 J Street
Modesto, CA 95354
Phone (209) 571-6480
Fax (209) 549-1140

Stockton-San Joaquin County Mexican-
American C of C
343 East Main Street #806
Stockton, CA 95202
Phone (209) 943-6117
Fax (209) 943-0114

The Bolivian-American C of C
P.O. Box 56104
San Jose, CA 95156
Phone (408) 272-2494
Fax (408) 272-9424

The Greater Moreno Valley Hispanic C of C
24371 Sunnymead Blvd., Suite C
Moreno Valley, CA 92553
Phone (909) 485-8170
Fax (909) 485-6918

The National Association of Hispanic
Real Estate Professionals
404 Camino De Rio South
Suite 602 San Diego CA 92108
Phone (619) 686-4050
Fax (616) 297-3229

Tulare Kings Hispanic C of C
711 North Court Street, Suite C
Visalia, CA 93291

Phone (559) 734-6020
Fax (559) 734-6021

Colorado

Colorado Association of Hispanic Real
Estate Professionals
3480 West 38th Avenue
Denver, CO 80211
Phone (303) 458-1345
Fax (303) 458-0757

Denver Hispanic C of C
924 West Colfax Avenue
Denver, CO 80204
Phone (303) 534-7783
Fax (303) 595-8977

Hispanic C of C of Colorado Springs
912 North Circle Dr., Suite 203
Colorado Springs Co, 80909
Phone (719) 635-5001
Fax (719) 635-6311

Latino C of C of Pueblo
215 South Victoria Avenue
Pueblo, CO 81003
Phone (719) 542-5513
Fax (719) 542-4657

Connecticut

Greater Stamford Hispanic C of C, Inc.
465 Canal Street
P.O. Box 4153
Stamford, CT 06907
Phone (203) 359-2050
Fax (203) 359-4153

Hispanic C of C of Greater Waterbury, Inc.
451 Meriden Road
Waterbury 06705
Phone (203) 759-0939
Fax (203) 596-2276

Florida

American Venezuelan Business League
10773 NW 58 Street #124
Miami, FL 33178
Phone (305) 894-4811
Fax (305) 436-7698

Argentine-Florida C of C
2666 Brickell Avenue, 3rd Floor
Miami, FL 33129
Phone (305) 858-1516
Fax (305) 858-3767

Colombian American C of C U.S.A.
312 Minorca Avenue
Coral Gables Fl 33134
Phone (305) 446-2542
Fax (305) 398-0545

Florida State Hispanic C of C
13876 SW 56th Street, #466
Jacksonville FL 33175
Phone (786) 221-2199
Fax (786) 221-2199

Hialeah C of C & Industries
1840 West 49th Street, Suite 700
Hialeah, FL 33012
Phone (305) 828-9898
Fax (305) 828-9777

Naples Hispanic C of C, Inc.
2740 Bayshore Drive, Unit 5
Naples, FL 34112
Phone (239) 774-4300
Fax (239) 774-9293

Hispanic C of C of Metro Orlando
315 East Robinson Street, Suite 190
Orlando, FL 32801
Phone (407) 428-5870
Fax (407) 428-5871

Hispanic C of C of Palm Beach County
33420 Clematis Street 2nd Floor
West Palm Beach, FL 33401
Phone (561) 832-1986
Fax (561) 361-1891

Hispanic C of C of Palm Beach County
420 Clematis Street, 2nd Floor
West Palm Beach, FL 33401
Phone (561) 832-1986
Fax (407) 832-1891

Latin C of C of Broward County
8320 West Sunrise Blvd., Suite 206
Plantation, FL 33322
Phone (954) 625-6616
Fax (954) 625-6693

Latin C of C of Lower Key West
P.O. Box 629
Key West, FL 33041
Phone (305) 294-6156

Nicaraguan–American C of C
175 Fontainbleau Blvd., Suite 1R-10
Miami, FL 33172
Phone (305) 599-2737
Fax (305) 220-1841

Puerto Rican C of C of South Florida
3550 Biscayne Blvd., Suite 306
Miami, FL 33137
Phone (305) 571-8006
Fax (305) 571-8007

South Florida Hispanic C of C
301 Arthur Godfrey Road, Suite 304
Miami Beach, FL 33140
Phone (305) 534-1903
Fax (305) 534-8365

Southwest Florida Hispanic C of C
10051 McGregor Blvd., Suite 204
Fort Myers, FL 33919
Phone (239) 418-1441
Fax (239) 418-1475

Tampa Bay Hispanic C of C
4023 North Armenia Avenue, Suite 101
Tampa, FL 33607
Phone (813) 414-9411
Fax (813) 414-0811

The Spain-U.S. C of C
1221 Brickell Ave, Suite 1000
Miami, FL 33131
Phone (305) 358-5988
Fax (305) 358-6844

Georgia

Georgia Hispanic C of C
2801 Buford Highway, Suite 500
Atlanta, GA 30329
Phone (404) 929-9998
Fax (404) 929-9908

Hawaii

Hawaii Hispanic C of C
P.O. Box 235263
Honolulu, HI 96823
Phone (808) 545-4344
Fax (808) 521-1496

Idaho

Hispanic Business Association
315 Stampede Drive
Nampa, ID 83687
Phone (208) 463-4226
Fax (208) 442-6801

Illinois

47th Street C of C
1646 West 47th Street
Chicago, IL 60609
Phone (773) 579-1200
Fax (773) 579-1986

Aurora Hispanic C of C
P.O. Box 7111
Aurora, IL 60507
Phone (630) 264-2422
Fax (630) 892-8013

Cermak Road C of C & Industry
2000 West Cermak, 2nd Floor
Chicago, IL 60608
Phone (773) 843-9738
Fax (773) 893-9739

Cuban American C of C
3330 North Ashland Avenue
Chicago, IL 60657
Phone (773) 248-2400
Fax (773) 248-6437

Guatemalan C of C
2814 North Kedzie Avenue
Chicago, IL 60618
Phone (773) 227-7330
Fax (773) 227-7379

Hispanic Business Assoc., Cicero C of C
5801 West Cermak Rd., 2nd Floor
Cicero, IL 60804
Phone (708) 863-6000
Fax (708) 863 8981

Illinois Hispanic C of C, DBA
33 North LaSalle Street, Suite 1720
Chicago, IL 60602
Phone (312) 372-3010
Fax (312) 372-3403

Latin American C of C
3512 West Fullerton Avenue
Chicago, IL 60647
Phone (773) 252-5211
Fax (773) 252-7065

Little Village C of C
3610 West 26th Street, 2nd Floor
Chicago, IL 60623
Phone (773) 521-5387
Fax (773) 521-5252

Puerto Rican C of C of Illinois
2450 West Division Street
Chicago, IL 60622
Phone (773) 486-1331
Fax (773) 486-1340

US-Mexico C of C, Mid-America Chapter
One Prudential Plaza
130 East Randolph Drive, 36th Floor
Chicago, IL 60601
Phone (312) 729-1355
Fax (312) 729-1354

Indiana

Greater Fort Wayne Hispanic C of C
826 Ewing Street
Fort Wayne, IN 46802
Phone (206) 422-6697
Fax (206) 426-3100

Indiana State Hispanic C of C
2511 East 46th Street
Indianapolis, IN 46205
Phone (317) 547-0200
Fax (317) 547-0210

Indianapolis Hispanic C of C
111 Monument Circle, Suite 1950
Indianapolis, IN 46204
Phone (317) 464-2254
Fax (317) 464-2217

Michiana Hispanic C of C
401 East Colfax Avenue, Suite 310
South Bend, IN 46634
Phone (219) 289-6846
Fax (219) 289-6873

Iowa

Iowa Hispanic C of C
P.O. Box 27052
West Des Moines, IA 50265
Phone (515) 453-8325
Fax (515) 727-1677

Kansas

Wichita Hispanic C of C
1150 North Broadway
Wichita, KS 67212
Phone (316) 265-6334
Fax (316) 265-6334

Louisiana

Hispanic C of C of Louisiana
4324 Veterans Blvd., Suite 205
Metairie, LA 70006

Phone (504) 885-4262
Fax (504) 887-5422

Massachusetts

Centro Las Americas
c/o Central Mass. Hispanic C of C, Inc.
11 Sycamore Street
Worcester, MA 01601
Phone (508) 393-8600
Fax (508) 919-007

Hispanic-American C of C
780 Dudley Street
Boston, MA 02125
Phone (617) 261-4222

Massachusetts Hispanic C of C
1628 Main Street
Springfield, MA 01103
Phone (413) 272-2221
Fax (413) 731-5399

Merrimack Valley C of C
264 Essex Street
Lawrence, MA 01840
Phone (978) 686-0900
Fax (978) 794-9953

Michigan

Greater Lansing Hispanic C of C
300 East Michigan Avenue, Suite 300
Lansing, MI 48933
Phone (517) 487-6340
Fax (517) 484-6910

Michigan Hispanic Business Alliance
645 Griswold Avenue, Suite 1500
Detroit, MI 48226
Phone (313) 962-6422
Fax (313) 965-6513

Michigan Hispanic C of C
24445 Northwestern Highway, Suite 206
Southfield, MI 48075
Phone (248) 208-9915
Fax (248) 208-9936

Mid-Michigan Hispanic Business Assoc.
108 South Hamilton
Saginaw, MI 48602
Phone (517) 797-8060
Fax (517) 797-8061

Minneapolis

Hispanic C of C of Minnesota
2308 Central Avenue NE
Minneapolis, MN 55418
Phone (612) 729-1138
Fax (612) 789-8448

Missouri

Hispanic Economic Development Corp.
1427 West 9th Street, Suite 201
Kansas City, MO 64101
Phone (816) 221-3442
Fax (816) 221-6458

Hispanic C of C of Greater Kansas City
1125 Grand Avenue, Suite 1803
Kansas City, MO 64106
Phone (816) 472-6767
Fax (816) 472-1252

Hispanic C of C of Metropolitan St. Louis
P.O. Box 78386
St. Louis, MO 63178
Phone (314) 771-4788
Fax (314) 771-4790

Nevada

Hispanic C of C of Northern Nevada
P.O. Box 7458
Reno, NV 89510
Phone (775) 786-4100
Fax (775) 786-4112

Latin C of C Northern Nevada, Inc.
50 East Libatany Street
Las Vegas, NV 89502
Phone (702) 385-7367
Fax (702) 385-2614

New Jersey

Camara De Comercio Latina De Elizabeth
603 Elizabeth Avenue
Elizabeth, NJ 07206
Phone (908) 289-0677
Fax (908) 289-6833

Ecuadorian–American C of C
61 Hudson Street
Hackensack, NJ 07601
Phone (201) 342-5741
Fax (201) 457-1683

Greater New Brunswick Hispanic C of C
P.O. Box 346
New Brunswick, NJ 8903
Phone (732) 745-5120
Fax (732) 565-7532

Hispanic American C of C of Essex County
P.O. Box 9146
Newark, NJ 07104
Phone (973) 484-5441
Fax (973) 350-9238

Hudson County Hispanic C of C
6000 Madison Street
West New York, NJ 7093
Phone (201) 662-0052
Fax (201) 662-8485

Morris County Hispanic C of C
P.O. Box 834 M
Morristown, NJ 07960
Phone (973) 644-3093
Fax (973) 984-3360

Statewide Hispanic C of C of New Jersey
150 Warren Street, Suite 110
Jersey City, NJ 7302
Phone (201) 451-9512
Fax (201) 451-9547

New York

Asociacion De Comerciantes Hispano
217-A Smith Street
Brooklyn, NY 11201
Phone (718) 875-1214
Fax (718) 875-1280

Bronx Hispanic C of C
P.O. Box 5400-57
Bronx, NY 10454
Phone (917) 213-3324

Caribbean American C of C & Industry
Brooklyn Navy Yard, Building #5
63 Flushing Avenue
Brooklyn, NY 11205
Phone (718) 834-4544
Fax (718) 834-9774

Dominican C of C
110 East Burnside Avenue
Bronx, NY 10453
Phone (718) 583-1900
Fax (718) 583-8021

Dominican-American C of C of NY, Inc.
825 Third Avenue, 11th Floor
New York, NY 10022
Phone (212) 709-0218
Fax (212) 709-0248

East Harlem C of C, Inc.
186 East 116th Street
New York, NY 10029
Phone (212) 996-2288
Fax (212) 987-2962

El Barrio C of C
1665 Lexington Avenue
New York, NY 10029
Phone (212) 860-2455
Fax (212) 876-5079

Hispanic C of C Queens
76-11 37th Avenue, Suite 203
Jackson Heights, NY 11372
Phone (718) 899-4418
Fax (718) 899-5998

Long Island Hispanic C of C
15 Atlantic Avenue
Lynbrook, NY 11563
Phone (516) 256-2483
Fax (516) 256-2463

Manhattan Hispanic C of C
P.O. Box 3494 Grand Central Station
New York, NY 10163
Phone (212) 683-5955
Fax (212) 683-5999

Mexican American C of C of Northeast USA
2710 Broadway, 2nd Floor
New York, NY 10025
Phone (212) 531-0552
Fax (212) 531-0064

National Hispanic Business Group
7 West 51st Street, Third Fl.
New York, NY 10019
Phone (718) 265-2664
Fax (718) 265-2675

New York State Federation of Hispanic C of C
2710 Broadway
New York, NY 10025
Phone (212) 222-8300
Fax (212) 222-8412

The Argentine-American C of C
630 5th Avenue
25th Floor Rockefeller Ctr, Suite 2518
New York, NY 10111
Phone (212) 698-2238
Fax (212) 698-2239

Westchester Hispanic C of C
P.O. BOX 80
White Plains, NY 10603
Phone (914) 328-7181
Fax (914) 861-1978

North Carolina

Latin-American C of C of Charlotte, Inc.
2938 Wheat Meadow Lane
Charlotte, NC 28270
Phone (704) 806-0106
Fax (704) 510-7470

North Carolina Hispanic C of C
150 Fayetteville Street Mall, Suite 110
Raleigh, NC 27601
Phone (919) 828-6087

Ohio

Greater Dayton Hispanic C of C
1 Chamber Plaza
Fifth and Main Streets
Dayton, OH 45402
Phone (937) 226-8209
Fax (937) 836-9974

Hispanic Business Association/Hispanic
C of C for Ohio
4115 Bridge Avenue, Suite 206
Cleveland, OH 44113
Phone (216) 281-4422
Fax (216) 281-4222

Hispanic C of C of Greater Cincinnati
P.O. Box 2593
Cincinnati, OH 45201
Phone (513) 929-2723
Fax (513) 583-1525

Hispanic C of C of Greater Columbus, Inc.
92 North Woods Blvd.
Columbus, OH 43235
Phone (614) 449-4770
Fax (614) 431-3885

Oklahoma

Greater Oklahoma City Hispanic C of C
4316 South Walker
Oklahoma City, OK 73109

Phone (405) 616-5031
Fax (405) 616-0600

Greater Tulsa Hispanic C of C
Bank of America Building
10802 East 31st Street, Suite A
Tulsa, OK 74147
Phone (918) 664-5326
Fax (918) 384-0096

Oregon

Hispanic Metropolitan Chamber
P.O. Box 1837
Portland, OR 97207
Phone (503) 222-0280
Fax (503) 292-3790

Rogue Valley Hispanic C of C
2311 Voorhies Road
Medford, OR 97501
Phone (541) 535-6277
Fax (541) 779-7669

Pennsylvania

Delaware Valley Hispanic C of C
Rd-2 Box 263
Olyphant, PA 18447

Greater Philadelphia Hispanic C of C
200 South Broad Street, Suite 700
Philadelphia, PA 19102
Phone (215) 790-3723
Fax (215) 790-3601

Pennsylvania Latino C of C
P.O. Box 11545
Harrisburg, PA 17108
Phone (717) 920-9920
Fax (717) 920-9921

Philadelphia Hispanic C of C
200 South Broad Street, Suite 700
Philadelphia, PA 19102
Phone (215) 790-3723
Fax (215) 790-3601

Pittsburgh Metro Area Hispanic C of C
425 Sixth Avenue Street, Suite 1360
Pittsburgh, PA 15219
Phone (412) 201-9140
Fax (412) 201-9149

Tennessee

Hispanic Business Alliance
7845 U.S. Highway 64, Suite 331
Memphis, TN 38133
Phone (901) 266-2999
Fax (901) 379-0825

Nashville Area Hispanic C of C
PO Box 41656
Nashville, TN 37204
Phone (615) 582-3757

Texas

Arlington Hispanic C of C
301 South Center, Suite 400
Arlington, TX 76010
Phone (814) 461-8815
Fax (817) 795-9499

Bee County Area Hispanic C of C
1400 West Corpus Christi Street
Beeville, TX 78102
Phone (361) 592-3315
Fax (361) 592-3315

Camara De Comercio Hispana De Amarillo
P.O. Box 1861
Amarillo, TX 79105
Phone (806) 379-8800
Fax (806) 376-7873

Centex Hispanic C of C
501 Franklin, Suite 806
Waco, TX 76701
Phone (254) 754-7111
Fax (254) 754-3456

Collin County Hispanic C of C
1515 Autumn Mist Dr.
Allen, TX 75002
Phone (972) 838-4567
Fax (972) 838-4572

Corpus Christi Hispanic C of C
615 Upper North Broadway, Suite 410
Corpus Christi, TX 78464
Phone (361) 887-7408
Fax (361) 888-947

Denton Hispanic C of C
P.O. BOX. 2536
Denton, TX 76202
Phone (940) 565-1919
Fax (940) 483-1917

Eagle Pass Hispanic C of C
438 North Monroe
Eagle Pass, TX 78852
Phone (830) 757-2704
Fax (830) 757-2703

El Paso Hispanic C of C
201 East Main Street, Suite 100
El Paso, TX 79901
Phone (915) 566-4066
Fax (915) 566-4479

Fort Worth Hispanic C of C
1327 North Main
Fort Worth, TX 76106
Phone (817) 625-5411
Fax (817) 625-1405

Golden Triangle Hispanic Chamber
3046 Proctor Street, Suite A
Port Arthur, TX 77651
Phone (409) 983-1169
Fax (409) 963-2329

Greater Austin Hispanic C of C
3000 South IH-35, Suite 305
Austin, TX 78702
Phone (512) 476-7502
Fax (512) 476-6417

Greater Dallas Hispanic C of C
4622 Maple Avenue, Suite 207
Dallas, TX 75150
Phone (214) 523-3402
Fax (214) 520-1687

Greater Hispanic C of C of Cornal County
904 River Oak Drive
Seguin, TX 78155-7044
Phone (830) 606-1805

Grand Prairie Hispanic C of C
114 North East 4th Street
Grand Prairie, TX 75050
Phone (972) 642-2621
Fax (972) 642-4116

Harlingen Hispanic C of C
2309 North Ed Carey Drive
Harlingen, TX 78550
Phone (956) 421-2400
Fax (956) 364-1879

Hispanic C of C of Greater Baytown
1300 Rollingbrook, Suite 504
Baytown, TX 77522
Phone (281) 422-6908
Fax (281) 422-6908

Houston Hispanic C of C
2900 Woodridge Drive, Suite 312
Houston, TX 77087
Phone (713) 644-7070
Fax (713) 644-7377

Kleberg Hispanic C of C
111 North Fifth
Kingsville, TX 78363
Phone (361) 592-2708
Fax (361) 592-8540

Lubbock Hispanic C of C
P.O. BOX 886
Lubbock, TX 79401
Phone (806) 762-5059
Fax (806) 763-2124

McAllen Hispanic C of C
P.O. Box 721025
McAllen, TX 78504
Phone (956) 928-0060
Fax (956) 928-0073

Mexican-American Network of Odessa, Inc.
1609 West 10th Street
Odessa, TX 79763
Phone (915) 335-0250
Fax (915) 337-6266

Midland Hispanic C of C
1410 North Lamesa Rd.
P.O. Box 11134
Midland, TX 79701
Phone (915) 682-2960
Fax (915) 687-3972

Pleasanton Hispanic C of C
P.O. Box 243
Pleasanton, TX 78064

San Antonio Hispanic C of C
318 West Houston Street, Suite 300
San Antonio, TX 78205
Phone (210) 225-0462
Fax (210) 225-2485

San Marcos Hispanic C of C
215 West San Antonio Street, Suite 112
San Marcos, TX 78666
Phone (512) 353-1690
Fax (512) 353-2175

Seguin-Guadalupe County Hispanic C of C
971 West Court
Seguin, TX 78155
Phone (830) 372-3151
Fax (830) 372-9499

TAMACC
3000 South IH 35, Suite 210
Austin, TX 78704
Phone (512) 444-5727
Fax (512) 444-5727

Utah

Utah Hispanic CoC
P.O. Box 1805
Salt Lake City, UT 84110
Phone (801) 532-3308
Fax (801) 532-3309

Viriginia

Salvadoran–American C of C of
Washington D.C.
927 South Reed Drive, Suite 9
Arlington VA 22204
Phone (703) 486-8700
Fax (703) 486-7800

The Peninsula Tidewater Hispanic C of C
445 Grafton Drive
Yorktown, VA 23692
Phone (757) 890-6203
Fax (757) 890-0596

Virginia Hispanic C of C
2810 Winterfield Road
Midlothian, VA 23113
Phone (804) 378-4099
Fax (888) 273-0248

Washington

Hispanic C of C of Greater Yakima
P.O. Box 2712
Yakima, WA 98907
Phone (509) 248-5123

Hispanic C of C of Yakima County
P.O. Box 11146
Yakima, WA 98909
Phone (509) 453-2050
Fax (509) 453-5165

Othello Hispanic C of C
646 South 3rd Street
Othello, WA 99344
Phone (509) 989-1147
Fax (509) 4888-3857

Tri-Cities Hispanic C of C
118 North 5th Avenue
Pasco, WA 99301
Phone (509) 542-0933
Fax (509) 545-2085

Red Mountain Cultural C of C
P.O. Box 373
Benton City, WA 99320
Phone (509) 588-4443
Fax (509) 588-5402

Washington State Hispanic C of C
P.O. Box 21925
Seattle, WA 98111
Phone (206) 441-8894
Fax (206) 441-9503

Selected Sources

There are many sources to help you with marketing to Hispanics.
The following are just a few that have been mentioned in the text.
If you would like your business to be included in future printings
of the book, please contact Paramount Market Publishing, Inc.

ADVERTISING AGENCIES

AHAA (Association of Hispanic
Advertising Agencies)
8201 Greensboro Drive, Suite 300
McLean, VA 22102
(703) 610-9014 • www.ahaa.org

AHAA's website contains a listing and
contact information for Hispanic advertising agencies throughout the U.S.

Cultura
3300 Oak Lawn Avenue, Suite 500
Dallas, TX 75219-6430
(214) 659-7700 • www.culturadallas.com

DEMOGRAPHIC DATA

Census Bureau
www.census.gov

Claritas, Inc.
5375 Mira Sorrento Place
San Diego, CA 92121
Information: 800-866-6520
Sales: (800) 234-5973
www.claritas.com

Woods & Poole Economics, Inc.
1794 Columbia Road, NW Suite 4
Washington, DC 20009
(202) 332-7111
www.woodsandpoole.com

MARKET NEWS

HWM Online (Hispanic Market Weekly)
2625 Ponce de Leon Boulevard,Suite 285
Coral Gables, FL 33134
(305) 448-5838 • www.hmweekly.com

Multicultural Marketing Resources, Inc.
286 Spring Street, Suite 201
New York, NY 10013
(212) 242-3351 • www.multicultural.com

HISPANIC MARKET RESEARCH

C&R Research
500 North Michigan Avenue
Chicago, IL 60611
(312) 828-9200 • www.latinoeyes.com

Nielsen Hispanic Television Service
(NHTI and NHSI)
770 Broadway
New York, NY 10003
(646) 654-8300 • www.nielsenmedia.com

Scarborough Hispanic Study
770 Broadway
New York, NY 10003
(646) 654-8400
www.scarborough.com • www.arbitron.com

Simmons Hispanic Study
230 Park Avenue South, 3rd floor
New York, NY 10003-1566
(212) 598-5400 • www.smrb.com

Synovate
8600 NW 17th Street, Suite 100
Miami, FL 33126
(305) 716-6800 • www.synovate.com

Yankelovich/Cheskin Hispanic Monitor
400 Meadowmont Village Cir., Suite 413
Chapel Hill, NC 27517
(919) 932-8600
www.yankelovich.com • www.cheskin.com

MEDIA

America Online
AOL Latino
www.advisor.aol.com

Batanga.com
2007 Yanceyville Street #224
Greensboro, NC 27405
(336) 510-5597 • www.batanga.com

LATIN MUSIC ON INTERNET RADIO

Radio Unica
www.radio-unica.com

Telemundo
10601 Magnolia Blvd. #12
North Hollywood, CA 91601
(818) 738-1516 • www.telemundo.com

Univision
1999 Avenue of the Stars
Suite 3050
Los Angeles, CA 90067
(310) 556-7665 • www.univision.com

*Univision, Inc. includes Univision and
Telefutura television networks, Galavisión
cable network, Univision radio (formerly
Hispanic Broadcasting Corp.) and
univision.com*

Yahoo en Español
www.espanol.yahoo.com

YupiMSN
www.yupimsn.com

MARKETING SERVICE PROVIDERS

Vision X (In-language call center)
3350 Wilshire Boulevard, Suite 300
Los Angeles, CA 90010
(213) 637-1300
www.vxi.com

RECOMMENDED READING

*Other books on this topic may be found at
www.paramountbooks.com*

*Marketing to American Latinos
Parts 1 and 2,* by M. Isabel Valdés

*Beyond Bodegas: Developing a Retail
Relationship with Hispanic Consumers*

Racial and Ethnic Diversity
from New Strategist Press

Paramount Market Publishing, Inc.
301 S. Geneva Street, Suite 109
Ithaca, NY 14850
607-275-8100
Toll Free: 888-787-8100
www.paramountbooks.com

Corporate Sponsors

Claritas, Inc.

Claritas, Inc. offers precision marketing solutions including demographic data, customer segmentation systems and other marketing tools. Claritas provides the Market Audit Survey®, the largest syndicated database of consumer financial behavior through its Integras division. Compiled annually, the Hispanic subset consists of approximately 3,000 Hispanic households. The information measures usage and balance information across dozens of deposit and loan products including checking, savings, CDs, IRAs, stocks, auto loans, student loans and mortgages, to name a few. Channel behavior is also captured to measure online banking, use of ATMs and more. Claritas is a division of VNU Marketing Information, Inc.

Claritas contact:
Carol Fitsimmons, (800) 866-6520
Sales: (800) 234-5973
www.claritas.com
Integras: (866) 744-1640
www.integrasconsulting.com

C&R Research– LatinoEyes

C&R Research has been conducting marketing research within the Latino segment for more than a decade. Recognizing the importance of this segment, C&R created a specialty research group, LatinoEyes that focuses on this exciting market.

The LatinoEyes division is comprised of a bicultural team of seasoned researchers who have lived in and conducted research across the U.S. and LATAM. The LatinoEyes researchers have exper-

tise in both qualitative and quantitative methods working on a variety of projects including brand identity and tracking studies, customer satisfaction, market segmentation and product development.

LatinoEyes adds value to your research by working with you to address your objectives and communicate important nuances about one culture to the other—we offer knowledge (not just data) about the market.

www.latinoeyes.com
(312) 828-9200
Miguel Gomez Winebrenner
miguelg@crresearch.com
Brenda Hurley
brendah@crresearch.com

Synovate Diversity

The Diversity Research unit of the global research company Synovate provides clients a full range of research solutions for all the major ethnic and lifestyle segments in the U.S., including Hispanics, African-Americans, Asians, GLBT and Seniors. We offer comprehensive quantitative and qualitative research, effectively and quickly offering a deeper understanding of the behaviors and thought processes of diversity groups. We publish unique and thorough reports on the consumer markets of Latin America, the U.S. Hispanic Market and a demographic profile report on the U.S. Ethnic populations. We also offer multi-client Hispanic omnibus research (TeleNación) that offers many of the benefits of custom research at a fraction of the cost.

Dick Thomas, Senior Vice President
Dick.thomas@synovate.com
(305) 716-6751

8600 NW 17th Street
Miami, FL 33126
(305) 716-6800
www.synovate.com

Vision-X

The Premier Voice of Hispanic Teleservices

An effective Hispanic campaign is more than just getting the translation right. You need to understand your customer. From Acquisition and Fulfillment to Retention and Service.

Vision-X, a leading Hispanic Outsource Call Center expert, can serve your customers from our 1200 inbound and outbound seats across the U.S. We don't just speak Spanish, we support it with in-language Recruiting, Training, and Quality Assurance. And over half of our workforce speaks 2 or more languages fluently.

Our consultative approach includes offer management, scripting, and ethnic database marketing. To make your campaign a success, partner with Vision-X.

LOS ANGELES | WASHINGTON D.C | MANILA | SHANGHAI

Bard Chodera
3350 Wilshire Boulevard, Suite 300
Los Angeles, CA 90010
(213) 637-1300 x6024
bard.chodera@vxi.com
www.vxi.com

Index

About the Author

You may be asking what makes me an authority on the topic. Well, I'll tell you: my expertise comes from the traditional as well as some not-so-traditional places. I am the president of Cultura, a Dallas-based advertising and marketing company specializing in communicating to the U.S. Hispanic market. We have been in business for four years. For six years prior to that, I was a researcher and consultant also specializing in marketing to the U.S. Hispanic audience. For seven years prior to that, I was the marketing director of a company that sold principally to an Hispanic audience. These things have provided me with a wide range of experiences and have exposed me to some of the best thinking on the subject.

What I believe makes me a greater and actually more complete expert, however, is that I can honestly say I am and have been every Hispanic consumer you could possibly want to talk to. To begin with, I am half Mexican and half Puerto Rican, covering the two largest Hispanic constituencies in the U.S. My father was a vice-president for the Gillette Corporation in Mexico. His world exposed me to the finest things in life and provided my family and I with a privileged socioeconomic status. In Mexico City, I was also exposed

to the world of influence based on family name and political connections.

However, way on the other side of the spectrum, my mother came from a humble background and from a rough neighborhood in Mexico City. All of this meant that as I was growing up, my weekends were a bit schizophrenic. Saturdays were spent going to the best and most expensive restaurants, while Sundays were spent going to picnics or to little holes-in-the-wall to eat tacos in some of the toughest parts of Mexico City.

This background helped me later on in life as I worked a variety of jobs. Once we had moved to the U.S., all of the influence and family-name value went out the window. Here, we were just like everybody else. There was no cushy life for my brother and me, although we did grow up in one of the nicest areas of San Diego. When I was still in high school, but old enough to work, I worked in a Mexican bakery owned by my friend's parents, at a body shop, and at a shipyard. In every one of these jobs, I worked with Hispanics from a broad range of backgrounds and origins. I lived in a privileged area with the sons of well-to-do Mexican businessmen and magnates and worked in rough neighborhoods with folks from the lowest end of the socioeconomic scale.

These were fun and enriching experiences that I would not change for anything in the world. I would love to say that I did all of this with the ultimate notion that these experiences would prove to be invaluable later in life. The truth, however, has nothing to do with a strategic vision and everything to do with how life goes.

Cultura

Cultura is a Dallas-based, full-service multicultural advertising agency specializing in the U.S. Hispanic market. All our strategies are based on in-depth consumer intelligence, emphasizing the impact we have on our clients' bottom lines and not by the number of awards we win. We are a collection of Mexican, Puerto Rican, South/Central American and Cuban marketers, poets, artists and business leaders bent on making our clients' Hispanic business grow.

3300 Oak Lawn Ave., Suite 500
Dallas, TX 75219-6430
(214) 659-7700
www.culturadallas.com